Twayne's United States Authors Series

Sylvia E. Bowman, *Editor*

INDIANA UNIVERSITY

William Styron

William Styron

By MARC L. RATNER

California State College at Hayward

 *196*

Twayne Publishers, Inc. : : New York

For My Brother
Richard Patrick
(1936–1970)

Preface

William Styron, because of his poetic imagination and strong moralistic convictions, has assured his place in American letters. From his first novel *Lie Down in Darkness* until his latest work *The Confessions of Nat Turner*, Styron has stirred critical debate over the nature and content of his work. Among contemporary writers, he is not only one of those most frequently written about in those critical magazines which specialize in fiction but he is also one of the writers usually included in college courses on post-World War II American fiction. Regardless of the critics' views of Styron's content, they generally agree that he has a unique poetic vision and that his imagery and descriptions are forceful and apocalyptic.

These images are the best examples of Styron's talent, and they demonstrate the influence of biblical and seventeenth-century prose writing throughout his work. The titles of two of his novels, *Lie Down in Darkness* and *Set This House on Fire*, are taken from Sir Thomas Browne and John Donne, respectively; but the evidence of such influence is stronger than that. We can observe the connection between his strong prose style and the moral issues with which he is absorbed. Like the seventeenth-century writers, Styron is intrigued by the moral implications of what Donne called "the new science which puts all in doubt"; but his concern is more with the effects of systematized society in which men are more absorbed with the technology and the weaponry of love and hate than with love and hate.

Behind the strength of Styron's mythopoetic vision lies a strong element of personal identity with his major characters. This sense of personal involvement is strongest in his later novels, *Set This House on Fire* and *The Confessions of Nat Turner*, in which the confessional-analytic approach is most evident and in which Styron makes use of his direct experiences. Unfortunately, there is a paucity of information about Styron's life; therefore, the more direct connections between his life and his work must await a more definitive study. For this reason, I have concentrated my study on Styron's main techniques and ideas in his works rather than upon their relationship to his personal life. Though I have theorized about the two sides of Styron's personality, I have based my view of his divided sensibilities on an analysis of *Lie Down in Darkness, The Long March,* and *Set This House on Fire.* In each of these novels he presents three personalities: a rebellious figure, a passive but sympathetic observer, and a representative of the system against whom the rebel acts. Only in Nat Turner does Styron concentrate on the rebel figure and begin what I believe to be the next phase in his work.

My plan has been to trace Styron's development from his early attempts at fiction to his later work. In each chapter about the novels, I have underscored the recurrent struggle of his central characters both to exorcise the demon of childlike egoism in themselves and to oppose a closed social system which regards them as vulnerable or rebellious children. Regardless of success or failure, each one of Styron's major characters makes an attempt to be free, and this struggle toward self-realization is his main theme.

In addition, I felt it relevant to include Styron's views on sex and violence and the way he connects them in his work with the death of love. Related to these subjects is Styron's use of satire and his sense of the spiritual malaise afflicting American life. Though some contemporary writers emphasize the absurd or comic elements in their fiction, Styron does not. He leans more to the satiric, particularly in his first three novels when his characters are, on occasion, more like myopic Gullivers than tragic or comic heroes.

Finally, I have dealt with the recurring but mistaken criticism of Styron as a regional writer who is limited to a Southern tradition and past. By comparing Styron's work with the earlier views and development of William Faulkner and Robert Penn Warren, I have shown not only where Styron differs from these earlier writers but also how he has created his own mood and technique and has reflected the contemporary dilemma of men operating without cosmic or social values. Above all these other considerations, Styron is more than anything else a remarkably descriptive poet. His use of imagery, particularly influenced by the Book of Revelation, and his baroque sensibility give his novels a different tone from those of his contemporaries; and in this poetic sensibility lies Styron's strength. In his novels he, more than any of his contemporaries in American fiction, with the possible exception of John Hawkes, approximates the poetic power of Herman Melville and William Faulkner.

Although there is a good deal of excellent criticism about Styron's work, few writers connect the theme and techniques which appear throughout his work, preferring to deal with particular novels. I am indebted to many of these writers and have acknowledged their work whenever appropriate. My main concern has been to present Styron's themes and the way in which he has progressively developed his unique artistic talent.

I am indebted to Mr. Robert Loomis of Random House for his help and interest; to Mrs. Josephine Haven of the Library of the University of Massachusetts for her inestimable assistance; and to Manfred Schollmayer, James Brannock, Brigitte Emmerich, and Klaus Schiller, staff members of the Amerika-Institut of the University of Frankfurt for their help in collecting material and for translations. I also wish to thank Professors Helmut Viebrock and Herbert Rauter of Frankfurt University for their encouragement and interest. I am especially grateful to Milly Fleming for her typing and proofreading of the final manuscript, and to Professor George Hendrick, whose criticisms and suggestions were invaluable. Particularly, I wish to thank William Styron and Robert Penn Warren for their encouragement. Finally, appreciative thanks are due to my wife, Margaret, for her patient support.

Parts of three of the chapters of my study previously appeared in another version in *Southern Review* (Chapter 2), *The Arlington Quarterly* (Chapter 3), and *American Quarterly* (Chapter 5).

MARC L. RATNER

California State College, Hayward

Contents

Chronology

1925   William Styron born June 11 in Newport News, Virginia. Son of marine engineer William Clark Styron, originally from North Carolina; mother was Pauline Margaret (née Abraham).

1938   Mother's death.

1938– Styron attended Christchurch Preparatory School for boys,
1942   Middlesex County, Virginia.

1942   Entered Davidson College, Presbyterian school in Davidson, North Carolina.

1943   Transferred to Duke University in Durham, North Carolina, as a member of Marine Corps V-12 unit. For a while was a Marine guard at Naval Prison. With encouragement of William Blackburn, English professor, wrote first short stories, which were published in *Archive*, Duke University literary magazine.

1945– Short stories reprinted in collection of best creative writ-
1947   ing by Duke University students.

1947   Completed studies for bachelor's degree at Duke. Traveled to New York where he worked for McGraw-Hill for four months. Enrolled in Hiram Hadyn's short-story course at the New School for Social Research.

1948   Short sketch "Moment in Trieste" published in *American Vanguard*. Began work on *Lie Down in Darkness* while living in New York.

1950   Completed *Lie Down in Darkness*; submitted manuscript to Bobbs-Merrill. As a first lieutenant, left for Marine Corps Reserve to which he was recalled during Korean War. Made forced march at Camp Lejeune similar to one in *The Long March*.

1951   *Lie Down in Darkness* published. Styron discharged from Marines. Short story "The Enormous Window" published in *American Vanguard*.

1952   Received Prix de Rome for *Lie Down in Darkness*. Member of American Academy there. Helped found *Paris Review* (spring).

1953   Married May 4 to Rose Burgunder (four children: Susanna, Paola, Thomas, and Alexandra). *The Long March* published in *Discovery*, No. 1.

1954　Returned from Europe with wife to Roxbury, Connecticut, where he began work on *Set This House on Fire.*

1956　*The Long March* published by Random House in paperback.

1957–　Wrote reviews and articles while working on *Set This*
1959　*House on Fire.*

1960　*Set This House on Fire* published by Random House. Began work on *The Confessions of Nat Turner,* a subject of literary interest to him since Hiram Hadyn's course in creative writing in 1947.

1963　Member of Board of Directors, Inter-American Foundation of Arts.

1964　Fellow at Silliman College, Yale.

1967　October 9, publication of *The Confessions of Nat Turner.*

1968　Became book reviewer for *Harper's Magazine;* received Pulitzer Prize for *The Confessions of Nat Turner.* Since 1968 Mr. Styron has lived at his home in Roxbury, Connecticut, and has continued to do occasional essays.

1970–　At work on a new novel, *The Way of the Warrior,* about
1972　a professional Marine. Part of the novel appeared in *Esquire,* Sept. 1971.

CHAPTER I

The Writer as Critic

I believe that in literature, as in life, ripeness is all—that creativity is its own reason for being, and possibly the only reason for our existence. That contemporary writing possesses a vitality and meaningfulness that will not be wished away. To think otherwise is to swallow a chic and treacherous myth. It is not the *Zeitgeist* that writes our stories for us, but human beings whom we know—from the distant shores of the posterity which we are—as Chekhov, Conrad, Flaubert. Some among us will be among them. That is not vainglory; it must be the simple fact of the matter, else we are already dead.

IN this early critical statement, from his introduction to *Best Stories from The Paris Review,* William Styron states a position generally shared by his fellow novelists, but one that is substantially removed from the general attitude held by a number of American critics in the 1950's that the novel was declining and that most current American novels were of minor importance. Styron's most forceful argument against this opinion has been his fiction, and his four novels have prompted an exceptional amount of favorable criticism from these same critics. Ironically, much of the earlier praise of his work was grounded on its similarities to that of William Faulkner.[1] While such comparison may be flattering, it often denies the writer the right to creative independence. Styron has exceeded the limitations of being a derivative or regional novelist; his four novels are the manifestations of a prolific poetic imagination.

In the early 1950's, many critics of the novel despaired of the postwar period of American fiction. Writers in such diverse publications as *College English, Life* and *Partisan Review*[2] apparently considered that current fiction was the lull before the void—the last effort of writers to continue a dying literary form. However, the critical response to attacks on the novel has been slowly but inexorably turned in the opposite direction in recent years. The most effective and valid means of changing critical opinions—the novel itself—has created a different atmosphere.

American novelists continue to produce fiction which, though it may be more introspective than inspirational, has created a more receptive critical atmosphere. Styron and his contemporaries—such as Norman Mailer, Ralph Ellison, Saul Bellow, and James Baldwin—have created in their fiction a new consciousness in American readers of the nature of their society; and it is one based more on a confrontation of the present rather than on a nostalgia for the past.

Confrontation of present reality is, for most contemporary American novelists, more than an assertion of existence, for American novelists have emphasized the values of awareness and sensitivity as the means of survival. In the earlier fiction of Mark Twain, John Steinbeck, Ernest Hemingway, William Faulkner, and Thomas Wolfe, the primitive or Romantic virtues are often contrasted to those of an effete and ineffectual society whose values are a mixture of Puritanism, commercialism, and faded Romanticism. Basing their criticism on the work of these earlier writers and their view of America as the land of failed promises, many of the critics of the 1950's found the frequently introspective, satiric, and the apparently valueless approach of many of the new writers to be lacking a serious literary or social basis.[3]

Although the contemporary novelist is often as compelled to point out the ineffectiveness of a Romantic view of America's past as he is to attack the commercial society (since both views obscure men's views of present reality), he is not without belief in some values. One of the central themes which emerges from the postwar novelists is that human values must be individually discovered, not merely accepted by men freed from their own and from society's pretensions. Ritualistic and conventional modes of self-discovery are no longer operable for men, and they are forced to rely continually on their direct experience. Socrates' dictum that "the unexamined life is not worth living" applies most clearly to these novels which, in part, challenge society's values but which more frequently, through the character of the introspective, self-absorbed protagonist, deal directly with the existential man. David Stevenson has written of the new fiction that its creators have "abandoned social man for the unconditioned in man" and that the earlier American fiction was "written for an audience which remembered a stable and an apparently purposeful world." He continues:

The new Styron, Bellow, Gold novel of our time, because of the Stygian chaos and old night in which it must be written excludes the morally or philosophically shy from its audience. Perhaps it has failed to capture the admiration of its critics, and the sizeable number devoted to the fiction of the twenties and thirties, because it has not been tempted (or able, now) to encompass the substantial areas of human experience which the very titles *Main Street* and *U.S.A.* suggest. It has not tried to create the large, usable social images of American life of these earlier works, whereby a post World War I generation of American readers, eager for instruction, anxious to lose a provincial morality, a political, theological, and cultural innocence, was led into a new maturity.[4]

In Faulkner, especially, the sense of the social past and the inability to find new values to replace the old order, even with its injustices, hinder his heroes from realizing their lives. His intellectuals are trapped by the past in contrast with his primitives who are not. But Faulkner's primitives have ritual and belief to support them in their enduring. In a similar sense, Hemingway's values, though lacking the profound social implications of Faulkner's work, center on a primitive code of behavior whose moral force lies in the awareness and confrontation of death rather than in life.

In contrast to Hemingway and Faulkner, the "past," for the contemporary novelists, often exists solely within the limited personal memory of their characters; but these characters are not neutral or disaffiliated. They confront inner and outer reality almost simultaneously. Ihab Hassan, drawing on Lionel Trilling's view of the "opposing self," extends its meaning beyond the idea of the Romantic ego opposing society to that of self-scrutiny:

But the contemporary self is also post-Romantic. It was not only born, like Little Dorrit, in a prison, and it has not only made of its prison, like Axel, a fortress and mausoleum. It has been also discovering the strange secrets of all prisons: that though their doors are never locked, no prisoner wishes to escape; that all avenues of escape lead to the same cell; that nothing may really exist beyond prison walls; that every gaoler is merely another prisoner in disguise. The contemporary self recoiled, *from* the world, *against* itself.[5]

Thus, the characters in much contemporary fiction are both inside and outside contemporary society, and we are aware that their failures or successes in being human are often inextricably linked with the failures or successes of their society.

Whereas earlier novelists were seeking values against the cultural background of the "American Dream" and its corruptions, a number of postwar novelists deal with characters who seek to regain a commitment to values in a society where, seemingly, distinctions are no longer made, where apparently there are no values. In much postwar fiction the characters, who appear in a world which they have not made and in which values shift continually, develop their own set of standards, not necessarily as a rebellion against mass society with its changing mores (since rebellion implies that there is an established order against which to rebel), but primarily to identify and assert themselves. Even if there is a rebel-hero, the source of his actions lies in personal identification rather than in any ideological belief.

If we judge these newer novels on the basis of standards appropriate to novels by Faulkner or Hemingway in which the protagonist comes to a resolution of his moral dilemma and in which particular values are reasserted at the end of the novel ("endurance" by Lena Grove in Faulkner's *Light in August* and Dilsey in *The Sound and the Fury*, or "grace under pressure" by Robert Jordan in Hemingway's *For Whom the Bell Tolls*), then some of the new fiction of Bernard Malamud, Saul Bellow, Ralph Ellison, and William Styron is unsatisfactory. As "examiners" of life, Levin in Malamud's *A New Life*, Augie in Bellow's *The Adventures of Augie March*, Ellison's unnamed hero in *The Invisible Man*, and the central characters in the novels of William Styron all develop in self-awareness either through reflection or through immediate experience: their characteristics do not change or develop so much as does their awareness of themselves as men of flesh and bone sharpen at the expense of the abstractions their illusions have made of them. These characters, though their experiences differ, often share a desire to free themselves from either society's definition or, more subtle and dangerous, their own illusory definition of themselves.

The search for reality turns inward; and, though too much

self-scrutiny often becomes ambiguous and frustrating, the advantages of the self-examined life do bring the protagonists to a true confrontation with their reality unhindered by illusions of self or society. Styron himself has spoken directly about self-confrontation:

A great deal of this morbidity and depression doesn't arise so much from political conditions, or the threat of war, or the atom bomb, as from the terrific increase of the scientific knowledge which has come to us about the human self—Freud, that is, abnormal psychology, and all the new psychiatric wisdom. . . . What people like John Webster and, say, Hieronymus Bosch felt intuitively about some of the keen horrors which lurk in the human mind, we know have been neatly catalogued and clinically described by Krafft-Ebing and the Menningers and Karen Horney. . . . I don't say that this new knowledge is *the* cause of the so-called morbidity and gloom, but I do think it has contributed to a new trend toward the introspective in fiction.[6]

This introspective awareness on several levels in Styron's characters is their dominant feature. Ironic awareness may paralyze them, as it does Styron's Milton Loftis in *Lie Down in Darkness,* or it may move them to action, as it does Cass Kinsolving in *Set This House on Fire* and Nat Turner in *The Confessions of Nat Turner.*

I Styron and Postwar Fiction

The work of William Styron is part of the new fictional milieu, but it is not limited to it. Styron is a writer whose range of theme and style make him neither a "southern" writer in the sense of being concerned with moral and social problems nor an "Existentialist" writer; he is, rather, a skilled craftsman with a poetic sensibility who shares the contemporary novelist's concern for moral values. It is Styron's unique literary gift of poetic descriptive expression which gives his fiction its main strength, not the general similarities in viewpoint which he shares with his contemporaries. There are times in his work when his intellectual and moral concerns range from the obvious to the hazy, and his tendency to philosophize limits his poetic powers. But when he is not didactic and allows his imagination predominance, he dramatizes his themes more than do pages of obvious moralizing.

For this reason, a discussion of Styron should center on his views of art, as well as of society, to clarify the nature of his involvement. In his criticism and in the themes of his fiction, he has aligned himself with the "new writers"—with their belief in self-confrontation and with their rejection of many of the attitudes of the older writers and critics. In Styron's experiences in creative writing schools and in his work in the founding of *The Paris Review,* as well as in his expressed opinions in a number of reviews and articles, we can find evidence of Styron's concern for the acceptance of "new writers" like Bellow, Baldwin, Ellison, and Malamud. Despite the critical accolades for his work, Styron has recognized that the limitations imposed on such a writer in the 1950's and the prevailing standards of critical judgment were often completely extrinsic to the new novels. In fact, he was personally affected, since the praise or condemnation of his work was at times based on its similarities to Faulkner and Wolfe rather than on its own merits; indeed, one critic went so far as to call *Lie Down in Darkness* a "literary pastiche." [7] There are similarities to such earlier writers in Styron's first work, but thematically and imagistically his fiction is markedly different from most of his predecessors in American fiction.

In discussions of his experiences as a beginning writer and in his later essays and articles, Styron is not as concerned with the significance of the postwar approach to fiction as with removing the critical obstacles to the acceptance of the "new writers." For the most part, he has been engaged in speaking against the limited viewpoint of the literary critics who have measured new work on the basis of comparison with Faulkner and Hemingway. In a handful of reviews and essays, Styron has indicated his views about other literary and social matters, but his best social criticism appears in his fiction. It provides a direct and even more personal commentary on the more profound themes of individual frustration and despair.

II Family and Early Education

Styron was born on June 11, 1925, in Newport News, Virginia, the son of a marine engineer William C. Styron from North Carolina. The elder Styron, with evident pride in his son's accomplishments, spoke of the boy's interest in words as a child; but he also considered the family's background to be an asset for his son.[8] Styron, the son, described "Byrdland" as the "absolute heartland of a deadened, unenlightened culture," as a world where the pre-Civil War past was still a reality. From the scattered biographical hints in interviews, he appears to have been an average reader and did not, he says, exhibit an unusual imagination. As an example, Styron recalled his first literary venture"Typhoon and the Tor Bay," which he describes as an "imitation Conrad thing," and as replete with sharks and a ship's hold "swarming with Chinks." [9]

He attended Christchurch Preparatory School for boys in Middlesex County, Virginia; and he once stated that he also intended to send his children to school there: "Most beautiful place in the world, first of all. Then it gives you something really strong and solid. That may sound trite, but I loved it." [10] When he was thirteen, Styron's mother died, and he started "going wild in that little village." Leaving the town and entering the school provided stability for Styron during a really difficult time in his life. At the small Episcopalian school, Styron wrote articles for the school paper, although not with any notion of pursuing writing as a career; and he garnered some of the experiences which he recounts in his first short stories and in *Set This House on Fire*. At this point, Styron was considering a career similar to his father's either as an engineer or as a draftsman.

In 1942 he entered Davidson College, a Presbyterian institution in Davidson, North Carolina; and a year later he transferred to Duke University as a member of the Marine Corps unit. At Duke, when he was seventeen years old, he first became really interested in writing. There he worked with Professor William Blackburn, whose students have included Mac Hyman and Reynolds Price; and, with this professor's encouragement, he wrote his first short stories, which were published in *Archive,* the campus literary magazine. They were republished in 1945 in Blackburn's anthology, *One and Twenty: Duke Narrative and Verse (1924-1945).*[11] The stories, derivatives of Faulkner and Hemingway, are typical products of creative-writing schools. As such, they are good beginning exercises; and, while they may not be strikingly original in character and theme, there are glimmerings of Styron's poetic capabilities in them.

III Early Short Stories

Styron's earliest published short stories give little indication of the kind of talent he displays in *Lie Down in Darkness* and in *The Long March*; for, with few exceptions, the shorter works follow a rather simplified story line with little use of the metaphors and the detailed descriptions that characterize his later, longer fiction. Since Styron is quite critical of what he terms "dreary little anthologies," and since he has never mentioned these earlier stories, we can assume that he is not particularly proud of them. Yet he achieved his first recognition as a writer from Blackburn, and this encouragement was vitally important.

The two stories Blackburn printed are quite dissimilar in tone and characterization. The first, "The Long Dark Road," is an account of a boy, Dewey, and his adolescent initiation into evil through a lynching. The story opens in a rural setting with Dewey's father speaking to his son of fishing, and the father's good-humored laughter sets the tone. But Roy, Dewey's evil brother, shatters this idyll by leading a lynch mob which burns a Negro before his father's store. The father's protest is stilled by Roy's horrible laugh ("a ghastly and fiendish travesty on the laughter of his father") as the men go about their deadly work. The shock of the lynching on the boy is reminiscent of the effect of watching the death of Buck Grangerford on Huck Finn, but the episode in Styron's story adds the awareness of the writer who, as third person, smells the kerosene, hears the innocent sound of the lark, and is counterpoised against the boy's sense of the evil sound of Roy's laughter. These sensations hang in the air after Dewey runs away from the scene at the end of the story, so that it is mainly the author's perception which holds the story together, not Dewey's.

Although the violence of the scene is reminiscent of other lynchings in Southern fiction and although the story is clearly derivative, Styron does show some skill in unifying the different sensations in the last paragraph and in giving the episode significance in the boy's life. It is apparent though, that before Styron could arrive at the varied levels of awareness which he presents in his later fiction, he had a great distance to travel.

The settings in "The Long Dark Road" suggest that even in his later work Styron's strength might lie more in descriptive narration than in characterization. The sensitive boy, the good-humored, brutal father, and the Southern country folk are fairly stereotyped; however, Styron is clearer and more direct when he describes the father's disembodied laugh, which reflects the ambiguities in his character more than his actions do. On the other hand, Styron has Dewey see the meat cleaver and the cutting block as both a gory Aztec sacrificial altar and a source of Sunday dinners—an awkward expression of the indeterminate nature of good and evil. Yet Styron was at least trying to present the complexities of the situation; and, while the story is not in a class with Robert Penn Warren's *Blackberry Winter,* we find in it an occasionally effective use of description, Styron's forte.

In portraying complexities of character, especially as Styron attempts them in "Autumn," the second story in Blackburn's volume, he is not nearly so forceful or successful. The story of the antiquated prep-school English teacher, Weatherby, confirms Styron's primary weakness in these early pieces, characterization. Weatherby's confrontation with his student does little to produce sympathetic characterization; and the "Joycean-type epiphany," [12] as one critic describes it, which Weatherby undergoes neither convinces nor involves the reader.

Styron had other occupations besides his writing while at Duke, and among these were his experiences when he was part of the Marine Corps V-12 program and was, for a while, a guard at a naval prison. When the war ended, he remained at Duke and was graduated in 1947. He then went to New York, where he enrolled in Hiram Haydn's short-story course at the New School for Social Research. Haydn, a novelist and critic, suggested that Styron might try the novel rather than the short story as a form. If Styron's early short stories are any criterion, Haydn's suggestion was excellent, for Styron's major weakness lay, as we have noted, in his characterization. In the larger range of the novel, he would be able to enlarge his characters through incident and would not rely on delineation with skillful poetic description. It was at the New School, then, that he began his three-year writing of *Lie Down in Darkness,* which he had originally conceived as a short story.

Styron's two other published short stories appeared in *American Vanguard*[13] (1948 and 1950); and, while they are not masterpieces of craftsmanship, they do indicate his increasing reliance on poetic description to create mood and theme. "Moment in Trieste" is honestly what Styron purports it to be: "a sketch." This Hemingway-like story concerns two Americans, Doc and Nick, who have arrived in Trieste by cattleboat and who enjoy romantic days of eating, wine drinking, and *amore* with two Italian girls, days that end in a tense dance-hall scene. Nick, the more intellectual of the two, while speculating about Trieste, Italia, James Joyce, and Dante, is interrupted by the contemptuous looks of the Titoists around him in the dance hall. Despite Nick's romantic illusions, the reality of the cold war upsets him; and, when he catches a glimpse of Dante who is regarding the "faded impassive face of Beatrice with timeless despair," he expresses his feeling of the impossibility of communication with the hostile patrons of the hall. The sketch relies mainly on physical description and dramatic situation rather than on psychological characterization. Tension is created through four brief scenes, one which describes the tense city and three which occur on the dancing terraza. Styron ends with the Americans escaping while the Communists are distracted. The slight theme of "Moment in Trieste" derives from the end of the Americans' romantic illusions about themselves and Europe—a subject which Styron examines far more thoroughly in *Set This House on Fire*.

Styron's last short story, an improved reworking of "Autumn," was entitled "The Enormous Window." In it, the central character, Mr. Jones, the headmaster of a prep school, is married to a sad little woman; but he is romantically drawn to Mrs. Temple, the school's business manager. Styron controls the physical description of the ways in which Jones is aging and the contrast between the animal spirits of the boys and his own frustrated desires more skillfully in this story than in his previous work. Jones's psychological struggle of flesh and spirit at least gives him more character than Weatherby possesses in the first story. Although Jones ends up in the absurd situation of the voyeur caught in the act, Styron's description has the curious effect of creating sympathy for his character.

Styron builds his narrative with a series of scenes—Jones's reading the Bible in his study, his lecturing Jeffries on self-discipline, his falsely accusing the boy of thinking of sex. While dreaming of Mrs. Temple as he lies in the grass, Jones's unfulfilled desire overtakes him as "an absolute craving to embrace everything about him." He peers through his binoculars at her house, only to realize that she is at the chapel and that the entire school is waiting for him to give the evening service. Later Jones, "witless with desire," climbs the trellis outside her house to see Mrs. Temple for the last time before she leaves; but, because his weight is too much for the structure, it collapses. She discovers Jones "spreadeagled against the rotting stairs," closes her window, and leaves him trying to pray, the sound of "a thousand tiny blades of inchoate laughter swarming about him, shattering the air like fallen glass." This description enlarges the dimensions of the action; and, no matter how absurd Jones's situation, Styron evokes pathos and also rescues his character from the stereotyped fate of the earlier schoolmaster, Weatherby. In this later story, Styron might have improved the content by not including the last paragraph, in which the student, Jeffries, encounters the disarranged, distracted Jones in the woods. If Styron had not underscored with this anticlimatic meeting the absurdity and pathos of Jones, and if he had concluded his narrative with his telling and just-quoted poetic description, the story might have been more successful.

But the "Enormous Window," which is far more craftsmanlike than Styron's earlier attempts, demonstrates clearly how he at times overcomes his weakness in characterization by poetic weaving of description into his rather obvious and simple narrative to give the characters and the narrative thematic unity; and how really skilled he is at this art is later abundantly proven in *Lie Down in Darkness*.

Styron's technique in these early stories relies heavily on repetition of imagery and setting. The characters are almost lost in the description of their surroundings. The narratives are remarkably simple; the characters are not rounded out or developed. They are ludicrous and ineffectual and are trapped in the details of their situations. To some extent this entrapment is even true of *Lie Down in Darkness*, in which the Loftises, in addition to their psychological difficulties, are surrounded by imagery of trapped birds and dark shadows. Indeed, the Gothic quality of Styron's prose is evident in all his work. Nightmare shadows and apocalyptic visions abound in his fiction and create an atmosphere of man's limitations and his despair. The atomic, dust-filled air that chokes the lives of the Loftises, the disinterment of Peyton's body, the dreamlike movement of the funeral cortege in *Lie Down in Darkness* all relate to the theme of despair in that novel.

In *The Long March*, in *Set This House on Fire*, and in *The Confessions of Nat Turner*, there are many scenes of detailed description in which Styron or his narrators hyperbolically express the visions before them. In the case of Cass Kinsolving, the protagonist of *Set This House on Fire*, he parodies Styron's prose in his moments of self-pity; at other times, he is given to poetic description, as in his visions of the hell of his isolation in an Italian brothel. There are numerous examples of Styron's poetic descriptions throughout his four novels, and they should be discussed in the context of each novel. But as a general point, Styron's poetic descriptions provide the unreal atmosphere in which his characters breathe. His technique has developed over four novels to a point where the excessive descriptions of his early work has diminished; as a result, we can see improvement in characterization in *The Confessions of Nat Turner*. Before he arrived at that point, however, he had a number of obstacles to overcome, not the least of which was his early success with *Lie Down in Darkness*.

IV Off to the Wars; *The Paris Review*

In 1950, when Styron was recalled to the Marine Corps because of the Korean War, he left his manuscript for *Lie Down in Darkness* with Bobbs-Merrill on the day he returned to uniform. When he was discharged in 1951, he received an advance copy of the novel; and he had begun his career as a literary professional with all the tribulations that follow. The sad but not unusual situation for the beginning novelist in the United States was especially true for Styron; he paid a price for being discovered too soon and for the kind of critical adulation which identified him as a derivative writer. This price was reflected, in part, in the critical reception of *Set This House on Fire*, a novel which many critics misjudged. For *Lie Down in*

Darkness was unusually successful for a first novel, and its success was partly due to the belief in some critical circles that there were no new Faulkners and Hemingways appearing and that Styron had mastered their technique better than most post-war novelists had. In fact, much of the novel's appeal was, as we have noted, that it apparently emulated the work of Faulkner, a fact best exemplified by Malcolm Cowley's review[14] in which he drew an extended comparison between Styron's novel and Faulkner's *The Sound and the Fury.*

After Styron received the Prix de Rome for *Lie Down in Darkness* in 1952, he joined the American Academy in Rome. Of his experiences as an editor with *The Paris Review*, which was born in the spring of 1952, Styron has written several reminiscences.[15] It was evidently for him a time not only of fulfillment because of the success of *Lie Down in Darkness* but of real potential. Styron recaptures his feeling for the "general great stirring," as well as for "the calm madness," in the air because of the international situation in his description of that spring in Paris in his introduction to the *Short Stories from "The Paris Review."* In the opening description, one is "highly colored by prejudice," and one is similar in tone to other reminiscences about Paris in the 1920's. In its fashion, Styron's account is as nostalgic as Hemingway's *Moveable Feast;* but, where Hemingway's account is characterized by often pure, hard egocentricity, Styron's recollections are marred at times by being falsely young and energetic.

Styron makes conscious effort to romanticize the founding of the *Paris Review* to suit the manner of ladies' fashion magazines. In fact, Styron wrote a brief article about the new magazine for *Harper's Bazaar* to introduce and sanction it for the ladies who might wish to sample intellectual life along with fashions. Styron's description of Peter Matthiessen suffices to give the tone of the *Harper's Bazaar* article: "With his equine, bespectacled, bonily handsome face, and with the lean and elegant cut of his clothes, Peter Matthiessen—ardent ringleader and spiritual guide of *The Paris Review*—often suggests one of those up-and-coming young English barristers you might meet in a good club on St. James's Street."

As for the magazine, Styron declared that "It was to be a literary quarterly whose chief aim was neither avant-garde, reactionary, political or neurotic, but simply to print as good writing . . . as could be found." [16] This intent is more simply and idealistically stated in 1953 than in the program that Styron presents in 1959 in his introduction to *Best Short Stories from "The Paris Review,"* where Styron appealed to a more intellectually inclined audience.

Through his connection with *The Paris Review,* Styron became associated with some of its writers and editors who desired freedom from academic or thesis articles in order to give more space to creative work. Their object was to establish a magazine that was, as Styron says, "pro-creative." In the Introduction to *Best Short Stories from "The Paris Review,"* he states the conditions of the time and *The Review's* objectives in concrete terms, and his phrasing and examples indicate his mood:

What we wanted to make of *The Paris Review* and what eventually it became was a magazine that most of the other quarterlies were not. Which is to say that we decided that we wished *The Review* to become a magazine in which the reader, hoping to find genuinely creative work, would in some abundance find it—stories, poems, art—rather than discover there one forlorn and lonesome story or a single poem sandwiched in between yet another tired, stale essay on Faulkner's symbolic use of light and dark and a desperate maneuver exposing poor old Herman Melville as a "manqué" sodomist. This was not an "anti-intellectual" position, it was not even anti-academic or anti-criticism. It was, however, procreative. (Only in this time of ours, perhaps, in which I once actually heard a respected critic state that "the critical function has usurped the artistic function," would I have to pause and explain that I mean "creative" to mean what it has always traditionally meant, i.e., productive of work which aspires to the condition of art; this does not include criticism, which may be of great value, just as philosophy is, but is not art. This is perhaps why monuments are almost never erected to critics.) None of us were yahoos or literary woolhats, we felt that criticism had its place. Despite the raw-boned American tradition against it, it is not necessarily a shameful act for a writer of fiction to read criticism. But one need not intend disregard for the valuable function that the best criticism performs (and here one thinks of a critic like Alfred Kazin, who seems to understand literature in terms of continuance and not something which dropped dead in its tracks with Proust and Joyce) in making the observation that when second-rate criticism begins to crowd out even third-rate creative work then the situation is not salutary.[17]

Styron, of course, indicates that the critic's function in a diffuse culture is to interpret a work of art not only in a traditional sense but also in its contemporary cultural setting. His objections to symbol-hunting formalist criticism are part of the reaction (first felt quite naturally by creative artists, and then in the 1960's by academic critics as well) against the constricting view of the New Critics. Despite his complaints against the academicians, he finds even more reprehensible the general failure of critics to do much more than wail over the decline of the novel—to lament that there is "no one to fill the vacuum" of "Faulkner, Hemingway and Co." And, after citing a number of writers, all of whom have become "established" writers in the 1960's—Jerome D. Salinger, Malamud, Truman Capote, J. P. Donleavey, Philip Roth, and Flannery O'Connor—Styron makes his case for the necessity to examine contemporary life, to trace its lines forward and back, but mainly *to confront it*:

There are no writers who today sometimes do not feel absolutely "drowned." But this is not a plea: it will be the death of writers when they exist by indulgences. The state of drowning, of bewilderment, of horror, of a sense of betrayal from all sides is possibly the healthiest situation in which a writer can find himself; so that if what I said before sounds over-sanguine it is not because the feelings come cheaply or easily but only because, together with those who founded *The Paris Review,* I believe that in literature, as in life, ripeness is all—that creativity is its own reason for being, and possibly the only reason for our existence. That contemporary writing possesses a vitality and meaningfulness that will not be wished away. To think otherwise is to swallow a chic and treacherous myth. It is not the *Zeitgeist* that writes our stories for us, but human beings whom we know—from the distant shores of the posterity which we are—as Chekhov, Conrad, Flaubert. Some among us will be among them. That is not vainglory; it must be the simple fact of the matter, else we are already dead.[18]

This statement is almost a credo for Styron and, by extension, for most literary artists in America today. For, whatever the cost, the "new writers," Styron included, are no longer bemoaning the loss of innocence, personal or national or social; but, accepting it, they are moving creatively ahead. As we shall see, Styron's *Set This House on Fire* traces this development in a man; and, whatever we may think of Styron's success or failure in this novel, the theme is inextricably tied to his credo of "ripeness" and to his view of the dangers of the "treacherous" myths of the past.

V Styron as Critic and Spokesman

After the publication in 1951 of *Lie Down in Darkness*, Styron, like a number of postwar writers, turned to writing articles and essays. In his earliest pieces, he discussed the dilemma of the younger writers and their struggle to free themselves from critical chains which linked them to the past; but Styron is neither so forceful nor so convincing as James Baldwin in his essays. Though they are speaking of what is essentially the same problem—the writer who wishes to express his personality and be freed from either critical or social labels—there is a greater degree of conviction and individuality in Baldwin's early essays about writing than there is in Styron's discussions of his own work. One of the essential reasons for this difference is that Styron in his early statements occasionally writes as an editor of *The Paris Review;* and his account of the founding of the *Review* and its hopes is, at best, a combination of romantic nostalgia, fact, and idealism which leaves something unsaid about the whole affair.

A number of Styron's articles reflect his personal commitment to his work and his right to question the critical standards of the past. In one essay, written a year after his graduation from Duke University, he challenged certain assumptions made by Diana Trilling in a curiously titled article in *Harper's Junior Bazaar*, "What About Writers Under Twenty-Five?" Mrs. Trilling had advanced the thesis, popular among American critics in the late 1940's and early 1950's, that young writers lacked a fresh point of view and apparently did little more than continue to describe with a good deal of horror and self-pity the atomization of the individual.

Styron, although in partial agreement about the lamentable state of modern fiction, differed with a number of her premises in his article, "Writers Under Twenty-Five," which was an introduction to *Under Twenty-five: Duke Narrative and Verse*.[19] He agreed that the style of Truman Capote, the honesty of Gore Vidal, or the anger of Norman Mailer are not enough. These writers' qualities do not overcome their faults: Capote and Vidal are apathetic in their treatment of their central characters, and

Mailer and Calder Willingham are limited in theme to "being against the system." But to denigrate such writers is to ignore their achievement and their potential, and what Styron objected to was Mrs. Trilling's weary air of condescension and her "wistful yearning for a brand-new moral and intellectual viewpoint . . . the very universal lack of which is a sure enough proof of its unavailability to the talents and craft of a young novelist." [20]

VI Styron and the End of Innocence

Styron does more in his novels than describe the further atomization of the individual. For, whatever failures or successes his heroes have, each of his rebellious ones comes to a point of recognition about himself and his true condition. For Styron's people have come to the end of what Tony Tanner describes—in his examination of naïveté and reality in American literature in *The Reign of Wonder*—as the operative myth: "The naïve or innocent eye was deliberately cultivated as an artistic strategy by many varied artists." In contradistinction, "the ordering power of analysis" is often lacking; for there is no attempt to do "justice to the attitude of wonder."

The world of childlike innocence and wonder is unsparingly attacked by Styron: in *Lie Down in Darkness* and in *Set This House on Fire*, immaturity is the major personal and social sin; and in *The Confessions of Nat Turner*, the attack is upon the concerted effort of white society to keep black men children. For Tanner, in much of the earlier literature, "Style is vision"; and there is the "interest in the naïve eye with its unselective wonder; the interest in the vernacular with its immediacy and concrete directness; and the effort to slough off the Past and concentrate exclusively on the present moment." [21] For Styron, this single vision is satirically parodied in the explosive and self-conscious style of Cass Kinsolving in *Set This House on Fire*, and this naïveté of "wonder" becomes the crippling immaturity of the Loftises in *Lie Down in Darkness*.[22]

VII The Tidelands Setting and the Double Perspective

Important to Styron's development as a writer were his impressions of his environment in the Tidewater country of Virginia—particularly around Norfolk, Portsmouth, and Newport News in the southeast corner of the state. His three major novels are at least partially set in this area; and, when Styron refers to it, he (or his characters) often expresses a nostalgic regret for the passing of another America. Although Styron's major characters are, like most persons in postwar fiction, primarily occupied with their present dilemmas, they possess a constant awareness of change and loss. We can draw parallels between Styron's settings and those of Faulkner's Yoknopatawpha, Thomas Wolfe's Altamont, or Sinclair Lewis's Zenith; for these fictional places also began as personal experiences for their creators and were transformed into images of a changing America.

In each of his novels, one of Styron's characters describes a setting as earlier twentieth-century American novelists might with a sociological awareness of change, but Styron often adds an ironic undertone which undermines the speaker's description. For instance, narrator Peter Leverett in *Set This House on Fire* regards his town with more than a hint of nostalgia:

To be sure, it had always been a shipbuilding city and a seaport (visualize Tampa, Pensacola, or the rusty water-front of Galveston; if you've never seen these, Perth Amboy will do), and in official propaganda it had never been listed as one of the ornaments of the commonwealth, but as a boy I had known its gentle seaside charm, and had smelled the ocean wind, and had lolled underneath giant magnolias and had watched streaked and dingy freighters putting out to sea and, in short, had shaken loose for myself the town's own peculiar romance. Now the magnolias had been hacked down to make room for a highway along the shore; there were noisy shopping plazas everywhere, blue with exhaust and rimmed with super-markets; television roosted upon acre after acre of split-level rooftops, and, almost worst of all, the ferry-boats to Norfolk, those low-slung smoke-belching tubs which had always possessed their own incomparable dumpy glamour, were gone, replaced by a Yankee-built vehicular tunnel which poked its foul white snout two miles beneath the mud of Hampton Roads. Hectic and hustling, throbbing with prosperity, filled with nomads and the rootless and uprooted ("Upstarts," my father said. "Son, you're watching the decline of the West."), the town seemed at once as strange to me yet as sharply familiar as some place on the order of Bridgeport or Yonkers.[23]

A setting such as this one exemplifies how Styron puts his descriptive talents to work on what is by now a familiar theme in American literature—the changes wrought by commerce and by urbanization in American life. It also gives us some of Styron's responses to the rapid changes in the life of the Tidelands and of America.

Styron's regret about the *past*, however, is a secondary concern of his work. His major interest lies in the resolution of the present dilemma in the personalities and lives of his characters. For example, the above description from *Set This House on Fire* is Peter Leverett's, who, in his speculations and conversations with his irate and bitter father, reveals his desire for justice and for an Apollonian order and meaning to life as opposed to the chaos and mediocrity of America in the Eisenhower era. However much Peter may desire justice, he lacks the ability to risk changing his own life. Like Milton Loftis and like Culver in *The Long March*, Peter may learn from the actions of the rebellious figure in his life (Peyton, Mannix); but he is hindered by his fears. In *Set This House on Fire* it is Cass Kinsolving, the Dionysiac madman, critical of American life, who has the vision and energy to change his life. In the presentation of Peter and Cass, Styron discloses a split viewpoint which derives from his own heritage and his own work.

In *Set This House on Fire*, Styron regards society through a double perspective and a double narrator: North Carolina mountain-man and Virginia gentleman. And, in a general sense, Styron is affected by this double vision, both as a social novelist commenting on the phenomenon of American life and as a writer whose characters are isolated and introspective. The North Carolina man, Cass Kinsolving, who at times is "possessed" and given to wild imaginary visions, is set against the conscious but generally passionless viewpoint of the Virginia gentleman, Peter Leverett. And these two contrasting characters, like two sides to Styron's own sensibility, appear in varying personalities or settings in his other fiction—in Mannix and Culver in *The Long March,* or in rebellious Peyton and ineffectual Milton Loftis in *Lie Down in Darkness*. This split view also affects Styron's descriptive imagination; for, in *Lie Down in Darkness*, the continual juxtaposition of fantastic visions from the Apocalypse with scenes of apparently ordered functions and rituals of middle-class life provides sharp contrasts of mood.

In Styron's first three novels, the double perspective of the rebel and the observer is turned on a third person: a figure (at times almost monstrous) who is the incarnation of all the corrupted or soul-deadening values of the social system. In the course of their rebellion, the rebel and the observer figures often demonstrate momentary resemblances to their opposite. In fact, Styron progressively moves toward an amalgamation of all three points of view in his novels: he makes the struggle more internal and psychological in each novel until he achieves his most successful work, *The Confessions of Nat Turner*. And this development is a logical one for a writer whose fundamental interest is in bringing his characters and readers to a point of recognition, to a new evaluation of themselves. But the best evidence of Styron's range and ability lies in the powerful honesty of the moral and poetic imagination which he displays in his novels.

CHAPTER 2

Rebellion and Despair: Lie Down in Darkness

FOR a first novel, *Lie Down in Darkness* was a critical success when it appeared in 1951. But much of its favorable reception by critics and public was based, as we have already noted, on surface similarities between Styron's work and that of other Southern writers, particularly Faulkner and Wolfe.[1] There is much more to this novel than what its original reviewers made of it; for it still stands, seventeen years after its publication, as one of the important novels of the postwar period. It is not difficult to understand its appeal to those critics who see the novel's function as historically and primarily social. In *Lie Down in Darkness*, Styron criticizes the society of pre-World War II. His characters are caught in a family and social situation from which they cannot escape. Peyton, the one major character who can see beyond the cage, cannot free herself and ends her life.

But the novel's real strength lies in Styron's unique poetic voice. In writing *Lie Down in Darkness*, he used the basic narrative of family tragedy; through internal portrayal of character, scenes of family conflict and of social satire, repetition of metaphor and poetic description, he has elevated the Loftises' sad history to the level of art. The difficulty of fusing all the levels of expression into a time structure was Styron's greatest problem, as he himself indicated in an interview. He has stated that he began his novel with an emphasis on character and that little of the narrative was planned in advance:

Styron: Well, the book started with the man, Loftis, standing at the station with the hearse, waiting for the body of his daughter to arrive from up North. I wanted to give him density, but all the tragedy in his life had happened in the past. So the problem was to get into the past, and this man's tragedy, without breaking up the story. It stumped me for a whole year. Then it finally occurred to me to use separate moments in time, four or five long dramatic scenes revolving around the daughter, Peyton, at different stages in her life. The business of the progression of time seems to me one of the most difficult problems a novelist has to cope with.

Interviewers: Did you prefigure the novel? How much was planned when you started?

Styron: Very little. I knew about Loftis and all his domestic troubles. I had the funeral. I had the girl in mind, and her suicide in Harlem. I thought I knew why, too. But that's all I had . . . Story and character should grow together . . . to give an impression of life being lived.[2]

For Styron, *Lie Down in Darkness* is essentially a tragedy of character, not of fate. Although his characters may feel tricked and defeated, they are not without choice and responsibility for their actions. And his characters are seen as portraits. There is a static quality about them; because they remain fixed in their basic selfishness, they are unable, like the birds in Peyton's soliloquy, to take wing and develop. Their tragedy is that their human potential to love, even themselves, has never progressed after childhood. The novel's episodes center on single explosive moments of tragic discovery which culminate in the Loftises' desperate funeral journey. To portray this tragedy, Styron has depended on the images of contemporary life and of the Book of Revelation. And the doomsday of the Loftis family has its corollary in the simultaneous explosion of the atomic bomb with Peyton's suicide.

I "The Man, Loftis"

The focal consciousness of most of the novel is Milton Loftis, the father. Gray haired, his young, handsome face gone to unhealthy flabbiness, he awaits the arrival of his daughter's body from New York. When the train arrives, it brings Loftis proof of his fate and circumstances, the result of all of his errors and of all his love. The death of Peyton is Milton's first taste of tragedy and of his own death—he is "confounded beyond all hope." Subsequently, we see Milton as a man who in the past has often been on the edge of awareness but whose sense of inadequacy locks him in the prison of childhood. Styron's description of Loftis's face is indicative of his limited range:

His face had become slack with grief, and as he gazed at the water his eyes wore a mildly astonished expression, as if he were watching the scene for the first time. He was in his middle fifties and had been good-looking in his youth (one could see that), and although some of the old handsome traces remained, his face had fallen into a limp and negligent disrepair: a young man's features distended into an unhealthy flabbiness, the skin over well-formed bones now full of big pores and deeply flushed. In his hair there was a patch of gray which had been there since childhood and which, far from being disfiguring, had added a flourish to his looks, a sort of focal point toward which strangers might direct admiring glances. About this patch he had been quite vain, and because of it had rarely worn a hat. (13)

Styron carefully begins by describing Loftis's awakening sense of tragedy but closes by shifting to the man's childish vanity. The description is significant because it foreshadows not only Loftis's psychological struggle in the early part of the novel but also his inability to realize his failure. This conflict between the mature consciousness of his true condition and the adolescent vanity which has obscured his vision is ultimately resolved when, in a moment of horrifying insight, he gazes into the pit of nothingness.

Loftis's "sense of tragedy" evokes his past particularly in the first flashback of the novel—one in which his father, speaking in archaic language, admonishes him that his youth would betray him. Milton Loftis, like a good many characters in twentieth-century American fiction—such as Hemingway's Jake Barnes and Fitzgerald's Jay Gatsby—is a case of arrested development: he has never progressed beyond the emotional center of his youth. And, though he may lack Jake's "code" of behavior or Gatsby's "gift of hope," he does have an awareness of himself which the others lack. His father, like a memory out of a Faulknerian past, appears at Milton's marriage to Helen. Regretful about obtaining the army commission which kept his son from combat, Milton's father tells his son of a friend's death in World War I. However, Milton refuses to accept the guilt which the old man hopes to make him feel. He rejects that guilt and the tradition on which it is based as surely as Peyton at her wedding rejects the artificial traditions of Port Warwick society which her mother, Helen Loftis, represents.

Milton despises his father whose ineffectualness and weakness offset his Puritan morality and fail to create a sense of guilt in his son. What the old man's remark does awaken in Milton is not guilt but a sense of loss for his friend, "the brother he never had, and of his father whom he had never known." (18) Since his mother is described only as a "vacant hovering face," Milton is thus seen as a person with no connections or past linked to family or friend. His father's religious statements about marriage are meaningless phrases to Milton; and, since he chooses to believe that his life is predetermined by circumstances, he has no sense of actual guilt or responsibility, only a terrible sense of void. Peyton's suicide brings not only thoughts of his own mortality to Milton but also of the vacuity of his own life for which he feels an overpowering self-pity. "Life tends toward a moment," he thinks, "not just the flesh. Not a poet or a thief, I could never exercise free will (15). In this way he rationalizes himself into irresponsibility. It occurs to him "that in this world there was no way of telling right from wrong," and he feels "safe in the all inclusive logic of determinism" and in the "sophomoric fatalism" (96–97) which his father condemned.

Whether Milton realizes it or not, his daughter's rebellion against her mother's values is an extension of his own hidden resentment against morality. Milton's fraternity-style rebellion is quite conventional, and his affair with Dolly is even more so. But, in his moments on the edge of awareness, he recognizes what Peyton hates—the loveless, dead world of social conventions identified with her mother. Milton is the first of Styron's passive but sympathetic consciousnesses.

II Puritan-Romantic

Helen Loftis appears as the strongest of the Loftises despite her inability to love anyone besides Maudie, her retarded child. Compared to Milton, who is weak and vacillating in his dependency on his father, and to Peyton, whose life has no purpose or meaning, Helen seems self-assured and decisive. Instead of self-pity, although she is capable of that, her strength lies in a terrible pride which is composed of her military sense of order and her icy puritanical morality which she had inherited from her father. Yet, like her husband, Helen feels an emptiness in her life. Even when she is disturbed by Peyton's suicide, her feelings remain self-centered. As she gazes into her mirror, she tries to re-create the romantic girl that she envisions herself to be:

An old woman's face, she thought, haggard and spooky: And I not yet fifty . . . half a century undone timeless like the memory of ruined walls. She swept back her white hair, pressing it against her head with hands that were pale, nearly translucent. Beneath the shiny skin of her hands the veins were tessellated like a blue mosaic, shining like an intricate blue design captured beneath glass. Now she did something that she had done many times before. She pulled the skin of her face taut over the cheekbones so that the web of lines and wrinkles vanished as if it had been touched by a miraculous and restorative wand; squinting convergently into the glass, she watched the foolish and lovely change: transfigured, she saw smooth skin as glossy white as the petal of gardenia, lips which seemed but sixteen or twenty, and as unblemished by any trouble as those she had held up to another mirror thirty years before, whispering "Dearest" to an invisible and quite imaginary lover. (24)

Despite Styron's sometimes sympathetic portrayal, Helen is usually characterized by her bitterness toward Milton and Peyton and by her strong attachment to Maudie. In fact, just as Milton identifies with Peyton and her apparently free life, Helen identifies with Maudie, whom she considers the victim of Milton's and Peyton's irresponsibility. She, like Milton, who longs for the adolescence of his college days, has a strong desire to return to childhood, to the preadolescent innocence with her protective father. They try to fulfill their desires by reliving their youth in the lives of the children, Maudie and Peyton.

Peyton, an extension of her father's adolescent yearnings toward freedom without guilt or responsibility, is intelligent, willful, and free—everything that Milton would like her to be. Maudie, mentally retarded, remains forever a child; and Helen relives through her her own protected, insulated child's world. She jealously watches over Maudie, and she draws satisfaction from Milton's and Peyton's irresponsibility during the football-game and fraternity-house episodes in Charlottesville. While they wander separately through the pointless celebrations of the town, Maudie dies in the hospital. Her death leaves Helen bitter and resentful; she has no direction or purpose except to direct her hatred at Milton and Peyton. The child's death is linked with Helen's nostalgia for childhood, as we might expect; but Styron gives the scene an added significance..

When Helen remembers her dead child, it evokes a scene in which she and Maudie, looking at Norfolk harbor, envision the arrival of the colonists' ships, "the swell and dip of the galleon sails" (219), to another America, a land of nobility, romance, primitive magic, and Christian innocence. Helen envisions the scene for Maudie as a simpler, happier world which must end. The end of innocence and magic is best seen in the episode with Bennie, the Indian mulatto, "the old magician, old artificer from another country." Maudie, who regards him as a "lover, father, magic," knows instinctively "that such divine magic must come to an end like everything" (223). In effect, this section of the novel is reminiscent of Fitzgerald's "green breasted continent" and also of the irrecoverable past which Faulkner mourns in The Bear. Styron, who often correlates the Loftises' lives with a change in American life, makes it quite clear that this world, which is so movingly described as past, does not exist in the present, and that the nostalgic attachment to it inhibits growth in a person and, he would add, a nation.

Helen is representative, therefore, of two contradictory attitudes in American culture, of what Leslie Fiedler calls the Rousseauistic and the Puritan. As Fiedler states: "Not only in our literature but in our lives, we have shuttled back and forth between a romantic nature cult and a Philistine anti-nature religion." [3] Helen manifests this conflict in her nostalgia for a childlike Eden and in her puritanical attitude toward sex.

Helen inwardly remains the child of romance hoping for a return to the innocent vision of childlike wonder. It is a part of her that Milton occasionally glimpses but one which is totally unknown to Peyton. She sees her mother as the stern, unloving moralist whose pretensions to Southern ladyhood are pointless. In Styron's later fiction, he offers two characters—Templeton in The Long March and Flagg in Set This House on Fire—who embody the values of their society; but they are externally and less sympathetically viewed than Helen. Though her hatred and resulting cruelty grow as the novel progresses, Styron does not portray her as a totally monstrous woman.

The death of Maudie signals the end of Helen's dreams, just as Peyton's death marks the end of Milton's. Although the deaths of their children bring Milton's and Helen's lives together, it is only for one tangential second. Unable to respond to each other, Milton and Helen turn to Dolly and Carr, respectively, for love or reassurance. The two separate journeys of Milton and Helen, accompanied by the lovers who can never answer their childish hopes, converge at Peyton's grave; and the couple meet only to confirm the emptiness of their lives.

III Everyman's Journey

The initial chapter of *Lie Down in Darkness* serves as an exposition of the Loftis family: Milton's terrible fear and isolation, Helen's pride in refusing to join him at the station, and Peyton's terror and desperation that are reflected in her last letter. In contrast to the Loftises' views are those of outside society—the undertaker; his assistant; and the waitress, Hazel, whose superficial concerns underscore the anxiety of the major characters. Dolly, Milton's mistress, who accompanies him to the grave of his hopes, is representative of the various "props and crutches— along with all the whiskey and with Peyton—which supported him against the unthinkable notion that life was not rich and purposeful and full of rewards" (43). Her look of adoration and her worshipful submissiveness provide only a momentary stay against his awareness of death and of the loss of Helen's love.

Loftis, like Everyman, begins his journey to the grave surrounded by his worldly supports. His memories of his youth, of Peyton, and of his political plans are at first gratifying; but they eventually turn to ashes. For, like the birds which scuttle through Peyton's last thoughts in her letter and in her long, final soliloquy, Loftis's dreams remain earthbound; they are weighted by the burden of his past irrationalities, the ghosts "of things . . . done, things undone."

IV Structure: Bomb-Flashes of Recollection

Except for Helen, the sense of the social and cultural past does not weigh on Styron's characters, nor do they evaluate their past lives so much as relive them in memory. They have learned nothing, and the flashbacks are really projections of scenes on the screen of present actions; as a result, they are not so much recollections but actual scenes in a chronological sense. Typically, Styron presents a sequence of immediately powerful episodes from the past and follows them with flashes of reflection by the characters, making the past into present. Each scene, a small drama in itself, ends with an explosive climax. The continuity is maintained during the funeral journey so that the lines of action are directed toward the central moment of the novel—Milton's and Helen's confrontation at their daughter's tomb. There was a risk of anticlimax involved in having these scenes juxtaposed with the funeral movement in the novel. However, Styron reduced this risk, first, by having the flashbacks ordered chronologically for the first six chapters and, second, by contrasting the futile meeting of the Loftises with the apocalyptic imagery of Peyton's reburial, her desperate soliloquy, and the Negro revivalist meeting in the last chapter.

In the smaller flashbacks within the first six chapters, Styron displays his skill in narrative structure.[4] Each section in the first two chapters is carefully prepared to present incidents of characterization and exposition of the family's tragedy. The basis for the next chapters is carefully established in the lawn scene at the end of the second chapter. Later, in her soliloquy, Peyton envisages her flightless birds waddling across this same lawn where Milton and Dolly began their flirtation and where Helen first felt her hatred for Peyton. In the third chapter, Peyton's sixteenth birthday party, she is bitter toward her mother for chastising her drinking; and she is emotionally shocked by her father's marital infidelity. The party, which begins as a gay affair of lights and music, ends in bitterness and sadness for the family.

These early incidents—the loss of manhood for Milton when Helen attacks him from her position of moral superiority; Helen's loss of Milton's love when he tries to recoup his loss by seducing Dolly; and Peyton's loss of innocence, her "look of desolation" as she lies silently clutching another child in the abandoned playground—bring us to their natural conclusion. Time swings back to the present, and Dolly's inane question "Where are we going?"—against the background shouts of the

Negroes who are pressing on to Daddy Faith's meeting at the close of Chapter Three—underscores the choice between childish despair and childish faith, neither of which is satisfactory.

Chapter Five introduces Carey Carr, the liberal Episcopalian, to whom Helen turns as she would to her father. But, instead of providing the moral reassurances of her soldier father, "Blood and Jesus" Peyton, Carey responds to Helen's attacks on Milton's adultery and to Peyton's incestuous behavior by treating Helen as a pathetic case of sexual frustration. Strongly attracted to her, he desires to convert her to his religion of reason and love. To exorcise the demons of jealousy in her mind, Carr suggests she read Montaigne's essay "On Some Lines from Virgil," a treatise on the necessity for the open proclamation of love, especially in later years, and on the "use and interest of marriage." In the interview with Carey, Helen conducts herself calmly; but her concealed desperation explodes in the subsequent scene in the tearoom with Dolly. Beginning in a subdued manner, Helen quickly loses her control because of Dolly's indifference to her accusation. Her scene with Dolly, as with her exchanges with Peyton and Milton, ends in frustration and defeat for Helen. Alone with her guilt and loneliness, she awaits Carey's arrival to drive her to Peyton's burial.

Incidents increase in number and intensity in the following chapter, which centers on the family debacle in Charlottesville. Milton's failure to reach Peyton with the news of Maudie's illness and his drunken wanderings ("away from his colossal responsibilities") through the fraternity party and football game are violent preludes to Helen's terrible wrath, which falls on both Loftis and Peyton. Helen's hatred and moral righteousness drive Peyton into sexual promiscuity, just as her attack on Milton drove him to adultery. The characters act on one another and themselves to force the tragic end.

In the final scene of Chapter Five, Peyton and Dick "lie down in the darkness," the action which indicates for all the characters—Milton, with whiskey; Helen, with nembutal; and even Maudie, forever a child—a withdrawal from reality. Dreaming "loveless dreams" after the act of love, Peyton and Dick are untouched by the radio with its news of the war, just as they are unaffected by each other. Styron writes: "They were painted with fire, like those fallen children who live and breathe and soundlessly scream and whose souls blaze forever" (236). The torture of their self-conscious and hellish loneliness is expressed in Styron's poetic image. Their fiery torture is intensified by their soundless screams. The apocalyptic imagery intensifies as the novel develops.

By the next chapter, Styron has brought his narrative to the point where the major characters and their dramatic situation need no additional elaboration. Peyton's suicide and the confrontation are all that can result. The opening scene brings the two journeys together as Carey and Helen stop at the same gas station at which the hearse is being repaired. In the station, Milton and Carey discuss Milton's return to Helen and the impossibility of it, a scene which Styron frames with a country-music song about Lazarus's return from the dead. The setting reflects the dead center of their lives. Loftis stares out the window, "clutching a beer bottle with both hands, in a kind of sacramental embrace"; and, when Carey pulls it away, Milton confronts him with a face "like a frightened baby's sucking on a nipple" (242). Carey sees the hopelessness of reaching Milton through his defensive wall of self-pity, though he can sympathize with Milton's misery.

Peyton's wedding, the last ritual which brings the family together before her funeral, contains within its explosive scenes the climax of Styron's novel. At first seen through Carey's memory, the wedding preparations begin optimistically—Milton and Helen are drawn together by Maudie's death and by Peyton's impending marriage. The calm is unsettled when the father and daughter, like secretive children, have a drink in her room, where she reveals her hatred for Helen and for the social rite of the wedding.

Peyton's feeling, her inability to be free of the ghosts of a past that holds them all; Milton's experiencing all the desires of childhood—hunger, thirst, the bathroom—while watching Peyton's wedding; and Helen's emanating her jealous hatred of Peyton and desire for vengeance—these are Styron's "children" who remember, who are destroyed, and who have the worst of both the child's and the adult's world: immaturity and spiteful memory.

V The Web of the Past

The consequences of the past actions and present feelings only lead to the inevitable disaster. When Milton tries to embrace Peyton, she rejects him; and Helen, seizing on this rejection, attacks her. The scene dissolves into the chaos of Helen's nightmare fantasy of a city of faceless female corpses, her ghoulish but eerily satisfying walk with a man, and her mad dream of Carey and his "stick." At the end, as Peyton confronts Helen and attacks her mother's hatred of men while claiming her own freedom, she speaks in ignorance. The irony is that Peyton is as trapped by incestuous love for her father as Helen is. Helen's knowledge of men, other than her godlike father—first, as an adolescent discovering that men were not all heroes; second, as a woman incapable of maturing beyond the moment of this discovery—closely parallels Peyton's experience. Thus Helen's repression and Peyton's promiscuity stem from similar experiences with men, who are represented by Milton. As if to underscore this knowledge, Styron shows Milton's inadequacy at the end of the wedding when, crushed by Peyton's disdain, he salvages his ego by telephoning Dolly.

Styron's picture is harsh and unremitting. Matters almost reach a point where only the hopelessness of the situation, not the characters, evinces the reader's sympathy. At the end of this scene, we are at the very center of Styron's inferno.

VI The Day of Revelation

Styron's final chapter begins, as does his first, with a factual description of a place. But, whereas Port Warwick is the land of the living, Potter's Field is the land of the nameless dead. And as Port Warwick is, in part, representative of the chaos in American life, Potter's Field is symbolic of its waste and decay: "The island itself is bleak and unprepossessing. There are islands like this, serving all sorts of cheerless but necessary municipal function, near every great city in the world—islands in the Thames and Danube and the Seine, and in the yellow waters of the Tiber. This one, perhaps because it is American, seems more than necessarily dreary. No blade of grass grows here, only weeds" (326).

To Styron, Potter's Field is more than that—it is the earth as described in the Book of Revelation; and the day is the Day of Judgment. Instead of Resurrection, there is annihilation:

The coffins are made of plain pine and these—twenty-five or thirty each week—are laid four deep in the big mass graves. There are no prayers said; city prisoners are used for the burying, and they receive a day off from their sentence for each day's work in Potter's Field. The other dead must be crowded out—those who have lain there for twenty years. Now they are bones and dust and, taking up valuable space, must be removed. Not just twice dead like the relics beneath Washington Square, they become triply annihilated: the prisoners won't let them rest, remove them—bones, rotted cerement and rattling skull—and throw them in a smaller hole, where they take up one tenth the space they did twenty years before. The new coffins are laid in precisely, tagged and numbered; in this way many souls occupy, undisturbed, their own six feet of earth for two decades.

Then all is done. The grave is covered. The prisoners load up their spades and picks, climb back into the police van, and are driven away. On a promontory near the sea the old coffins are burning, for these too must be destroyed. They make a beautiful and lonely pyre; stacked high, they burn quickly, because the wood has become well decayed. Decay flowers in the air too, ripe and fleshy, yet it is a clean decay, as natural as dying leaves; decay is being destroyed. (327)

In this scene Styron is at his descriptive best, for he transforms the physical horror into a vision of the corruption of human values in our time. Through this example of his poetic imagination, he suggests more than a physical analogy to mass murders and atomic destruction in his imagery. Peyton's death and the mass deaths are the "promised end" that Kent speaks of at the end of *King Lear*. Though Peyton is not Cordelia and though Milton lacks Lear's spirit, there is a parallel in the daughters' deaths; for both are indirectly the consequences of man's selfishness and spite.[5]

While gnats cloud the air over the island with its sewages, human disposal plants, and general atmosphere of putrefaction and waste, Peyton's grave is opened so that Harry can identify her body. Then abruptly Styron closes the scene with a journey on Charon's ferry from the Isle of the Dead.

The next section is the weakest of the novel, for in it Styron breaks off the poetic-imaginative account of the Loftises with a flat, naturalistic description of the relationship between Harry and Peyton and of their experiences among Styron's New York intelligentsia. Though the details are necessary to make Peyton's soliloquy more comprehensible to the reader, this factual material partially saps the energy and pace of his last chapter.

The opening of the Seventh Seal, Peyton's last day, restores the intensity of Styron's poetic vision. Throughout *Lie Down in Darkness* Styron makes use of apocalyptic imagery, thunderheads, sudden shifts of light and dark in the sky, and the dust which fills the atmosphere of the Tidelands countryside with the pervading image of atomic destruction in the background. Specifically, Styron makes allusion to Abaddon (216), a name for Apollyon, the "angel of the bottomless pit" (Apocalypse 9:11) and to the opening scene of Chapter Seven in the novel; the continual use of bird imagery, often equated with ghosts ("the shadow of a hawk . . . a wraith . . . wings outspread like something crucified" (108), "children's voices breaking in upon her [Helen's] dreams like the chatter of remote, unknown birds" [134]): these and many other metaphors point to the last sustained poetic passage of Peyton's swan song.

References to the Baroque mood of the seventeenth century, a time of faith and doubt with which Peyton identifies in her conscious intellect, are naturally worked also into her unconscious and are part of a hierarchy of cultural values which Styron alludes to in his works generally. He often mentions eighteenth-century music, for example, as a representation of the order and symmetry in life which does not really exist. One example of this musical reference is Mozart's Papageno singing to Peyton (346) in her sleep before her first dream about birds. The music, like Peyton's clock in her soliloquy, gives a sense of order which contrasts with the chaotic, wingless birds.

There is a poetic structure throughout *Lie Down in Darkness* which can be described as a mounting, growing metaphor which enlarges the action through sound and image. This framework is Styron's own voice; it is not a derivation; and it gives more unity and structure than his narrative development. Like John Hawkes's work, Styron's defies synoptic or imagistic analysis since much of the effect of his novel is on the subconscious.

The still dust that blankets and stifles life in the beginning of *Lie Down in Darkness* is gradually stirred by angry memories and is replaced by images of violence and death as the characters approach Peyton's open grave. This choking atmosphere becomes more obvious in Chapter Six, when Styron closes this brief introductory scene with the "sudden sickening odor in the air, sweet and diseased, pestilential, like that of burning flesh" (246). Thus Peyton's last vision comes as the culmination to Styron's desperate poetry. Within that vision are the places and images of the past, the explosive scenes and the tortured feelings of the whole family. She is the bearer of their pain, the sacrificial victim, whose sacrifice is meaningless except that it ends the suffering.

The section begins with a prayer from Job, "I know my redeemer liveth," a phrase which Helen at times voices and which the Negroes echo on their way to Daddy Faith's revival. Yet now it is followed by lines which strongly suggest Judgment Day—"though worms destroy this body, yet in my flesh shall I . . ."; and, by omitting the "rise again," Styron mutes any expression of hope.

VII Peyton's Soliloquy

The section which follows is Peyton's stream of consciousness on the day she commits suicide, and the dominant images which Styron uses in the poetic section are those of wingless, hopeless birds; even the name of her apelike lover, Cecchino (magpie), is part of this imagery. The culmination of the bird imagery is Peyton's nude flight to death. While Cecchino prepares for his sexual assault on Peyton's sick body, she dreams of all the birds she has seen—Helen is perhaps a condor; Milton, an ostrich. In her "milky" dreams of the womb, the figure of Milton appears and reappears as Bunny, the object of her incestuous child love for her father.

With the recurring figure of Milton and the bird images, Styron gives us the basis for Peyton's love-hate relationship with men. Her nymphomania and her desire for revenge on her father and on Harry stem from her dependence on them and from their betrayals. In an essay on Styron, Melvin J. Friedman makes much of the clock image used throughout Peyton's soliloquy, and he discusses Styron's work in relation to other stream-of-consciousness novelists like Joyce in *Ulysses* and Virginia Woolf in *Mrs. Dalloway*. In those novels the use of clock images bears a relation to Bergson's theory of psychological time.[6] There are parallels to be sure, particularly in Faulkner's, Woolf's, and Joyce's works; but Styron employs the image differently.

Where other writers use the clock as a device to mark changes in mood and incident and to show the inexorable flux of time, Styron presents the clock as an image of the child's security of the womb in Peyton's inner consciousness in direct contrast to the physical pain she feels in her flesh:

then I felt it; the cramp exploding in my womb as if everything inside of me, heart, liver and lights, had been squeezed aside and I was all agonizing womb, crying aloud, gasping like a fish. "What's the matter?" he said. He came near me. I wondered if I was bleeding yet. "No," I said. "You done it last time. What's the matter?" I sank back again, watching the clock: 2:30, it said, and I could hear the almost silent whir, see the words Benrus Swiss movement, U.S.A., in a crescent around its rim. I said, "No" again, with a thought for the clock; inside, it would be filled with clean chrome, springs and cogs all working quietly; in there I could creep and sprawl along the mainspring, borne round and round through the darkness, hear the click and whir, my only light a pinpoint where the alarm button comes through, shining down on the jewels and rubies like a shaft in a Cathedral. (337)

The bird images, which I think are even more significant than those of the clock, are seen ambiguously not only as the family totem but also as the reality of Peyton's hope, experience, and, finally, despair. When she tells of her first dream of the birds, they are clearly associated with her physical and emotional insulation against men. The bird is seen at one point as a male sex organ and then, with reference to Dickie Boy and her father, as flightless birds: "Dickie Boy couldn't ever get big after the first time, he was afraid and sometimes he'd sob he was so frustrated, his bird was so small and futile. . . . There were birds in my mind, landbound birds whirling about, dodos and penguins and cassowaries, ostriches befouling their lovely black plumes, and these seemed mixed up with Bunny" (340-41). Again, the bird is an expression of another kind of reality, "Guilt is the thing with feathers." The conflict in images is between the clock, which is a metaphor for the womb, order, security, thoughtless innocence, a suspension of life, and the birds, which are meta-

49

phors for outer reality, insecurity, unconscious and conscious guilt, and the continuous chaotic flow of life.

Of greater significance is the idea of the birds as totem figures for the family. Peyton makes it evident in her soliloquy that the family totem for the Loftises is related to the birds: "I thought of Byrds. Grandmother was from Lynchburg, too; she had the face of an angel" (338). Yet a few lines before she recalls a one-eyed, lice-covered condor from the same town. The grandmother is the one who gives Milton his totem animal name, Bunny (like Peter Leverett—rabbit—in *Set This House on Fire* or Culver in *The Long March*); Milton is a passive and inadequate figure. Other names like *Carey* Carr and Ella *Swan* are also reminders throughout the novel that the action occurs in Byrdland.

The end brings Peyton's final flight from reality. Naked as a child, she has put away all the vestments of reality in one final attempt to fly free of life. Forced by her guilt ("Something hurries me through memory, too, but I can't pause to remember, for a guilt past memory or dreaming, much darker impels me on") and drawn by a faint hope ("Perhaps I shall rise at another time, though I lie down in darkness and have my light in ashes" [386]), she follows to its only conclusion, withdrawal from life, and lies "down in darkness."

Peyton's outpouring comes at the end of a novel filled with interior monologues and soliloquies, yet Peyton's cry is markedly different from those of the other characters since she is the result of their self-pitying, vicious, and unforgiving past actions. Of the three Loftises, she is the least responsible; and Styron so indicates in his treatment of her monologue. As Henry James does with Nanda Brookenham in *The Awkward Age*, Styron presents Peyton first through the memories of Milton and Helen who fail to know her. Though we have a general idea of her character and motivations before the soliloquy, Peyton is not really understood until the monologue which reveals her incestuous love for Milton. Her terror and madness as well as her sense of drowning are given without comment in contrast to Styron's treatment of Milton and Helen. Their memories are colored by their delusions and self-pity; Peyton's, by her child's desires and frustrations.

In contrast to Peyton's futile suicide, we have the figure in Harry's painting of a rabbi-monk ("gazing ceaselessly upward toward his own ascending spirit" [378]) against a dead, forlorn landscape. Peyton is, however, beyond faith; and, tortured by guilt and her inability to forgive, she destroys Harry's last vestige of love and forgiveness for her by accusing him of betrayal: "Oh, I would say, you've never understood me, Harry, that not out of vengeance have I accomplished all my sins but because something has always been close to dying in my soul, and I've sinned only in order to lie down in darkness and find, somewhere in the net of dreams, a new father, a new home" (379). Peyton's net of dreams, like those of her ineffectual parents, holds her earthbound. "Oh must" is her last compulsive cry before her suicide.

VIII The Denouement

The last scenes of *Lie Down in Darkness* are a necessary denouement. Helen's insanity becomes openly evident. In a scene drowned in rain, she momentarily seems reconciled to Milton; and then, still revengeful because of Peyton, she turns from him in her maniacal pride and leaves him with nothing.

The Negro revivalists provide an ironic choral commentary to the end of Styron's Euripidean tragedy. Throughout the novel, Styron works in a motif of Negroes as people in bondage who mutely observe the whites' tortured lives. They are often seen carrying burdens or helping whites, as when a Negro helps Milton out of the ditch he has drunkenly fallen into in the Charlottesville episode. As the novel concludes, the Negroes' strength is reflected in Ella Swan's stoic grief over Peyton and also in the sense of collective strength that the Negroes feel against the lone white man in the bus going to the revival site.

The appearance of Daddy Faith, however, brings about a curious close to Styron's Book of Revelation; for, instead of the trumpet's announcing the opening of the Seventh Seal, it announces the appearance of Daddy Faith. A religious pitchman who presents a flamboyant version of Carey Carr's effete Christianity, Daddy Faith supplies the Negroes with their father image. His message is filled with the clichés of hope—tapping himself on the chest he tells them the word of "your God shall stand forever" (399). He praises the war's end—and, as the dust of the atomic bomb is the central image in the opening of the novel and is significantly, even obtrusively, placed in the account of Peyton's last day, it also is a subject for Daddy Faith, who sees it as a sign of victory.

In this way Styron presents a scene similar to Dilsey's section in Faulkner's *The Sound and the Fury*. He portrays Ella—her "face wore the passive look of one who has seen all, borne all, known all and expects little more, of either joy or suffering . . . it was because her outlook on life was basically tragic" (389)—as an enduring figure; but he then proceeds to demonstrate the sheer emotionalism of her faith. Her hysteria over Daddy Faith is ironic. Instead of the simple preacher of Faulkner's sermon, Daddy Faith is a showman, not a healer of souls. Even after his sermon La Ruth continues the pattern of puritanical guilt about sex when she punishes Stonewall.

The failure of Carey's religion contrasts to the charlatanism of Daddy Faith and his religious clichés; and the dreaming mood of spellbound Ella—transfixed by the train in her religious ecstasy—gives Styron's ending a prophetic and essentially hopeless tone sharply different from Faulkner's note of endurance. Religion, rationally or emotionally viewed, fails to supply what only human love and concern can render. The train "like the clatter of the opening of everlasting gates and doors—passed swiftly on—toward Richmond, the North, the oncoming night" (400).

While the journey of the hearse and Carey's car gives the narrative a sense of progression, the journey of the railroad train provides an outer movement of inevitability which brackets the novel. Initially, the train serves as an introduction to the social panorama of Port Warwick, Styron's staked-out township in Tidewater, Virginia. This area figures briefly in *Set This House on Fire* and is the setting for his last novel, *The Confessions of Nat Turner*. Here within the limits of the town are the wilderness, old plantations, shipyards, new factories, suburbia, and slums—a cross-section of the changing American landscape. At the end of the novel, the train provides the final apocalyptic blast before the "oncoming night" which will soon envelop Styron's wasted society. Only Harry comes through with any truly tragic awareness, and his voice is gone long before the novel's end.

IX Satiric Elements

Lie Down in Darkness is a novel not just of personal tragedy but of the disintegration of a society. The center of the novel is constructed around "four or five long dramatic scenes revolving around the daughter, Peyton, at different stages in her life," [7] but they are also commentaries on American life. Although these scenes exist in Milton's and Helen's memories as moments of emotional conflict, as stages in the failure of love, there is on another level a presentation of the Loftises' world and the social changes wrought in President Franklin D. Roosevelt's time. On this secondary level of social commentary there is a marked similarity in the Loftises' journeys to those in *The Great Gatsby*. Styron, like Fitzgerald, constructs his novel around a series of car journeys wherein the physical movement parallels the characters' frustrations and, by extension, those of their society as well. The physical movement is correlated with the characters' remembrances of social occasions which mirror the boorish complacency and immaturity of wartime American society.

In describing the "celebrations" of this society, Styron often changes his tone from poetic imagery to satire; and, as in his early short stories, he presents caricatures rather than characters. Styron once stated that "It seems to me that only a great satirist can tackle the world's problems and articulate them";[8] and, although *Lie Down in Darkness* is not a satirical work in the sense that *Set This House on Fire* is, Styron does present social scenes as background to the tragedy of the Loftises. The older, established society of the Cartwrights, insulated from the revolution in society of the world "outside," or the world of Tidewater, Virginia; collegiate life at the football game and the fraternity house, the alcoholic swirl of false sophistication and gaiety—both provide the background for Milton's scene of stupid drunkenness in pursuit of Peyton.

Peyton's wedding provides Styron with an opportunity to give a satiric account of American society in attending one of its most important rituals. The guest list reminds one of Gatsby's party-goers; and the ceremony, although subdued in description, allows Styron to comment on forms of secular marriage in American Society. The wedding itself, which ends in an orgy of alcoholic hate within the family and with sexual prurience for some of the guests, destroys the original tone of reverence in the ceremony and reveals the superficial cover of a community of selfish children. Nor is Styron's comment on society limited to small-town life. He extends the range of the novel to include the effete intellectual world of New York, one which is accounted in another "listing" by Styron when he describes Albert Berger as a Poseidon reigning over the drowning in his sea-cave apartment.

X Family Drama

We can find a parallel to *Lie Down in Darkness* in the works of some American dramatists who use the form of Greek tragedy without its cosmic significance; indeed, they are following the example of Ibsen's social dramas without understanding the nature of his attack on society. Arthur Miller, Eugene O'Neill, and Edward Albee use the drama of family tragedy as a basic framework, thus limiting the possibilities for a character's freedom. Something similar happens in the family situation in *Lie Down in Darkness*.

The basic problem in the family tragedy is that it sometimes restricts the artist to a kind of Freudian determinism which rarely frees the characters to go beyond the stages of childhood or adolescence in their search for identity. More specifically, the plays themselves are a way of freeing the artists from their "ghosts" as in O'Neill's *Long Day's Journey Into the Night*. The characters in these dramas, like the characters in Ibsen's *Ghosts*, are confined by "hidden forces" to act out their lives. In the plays of Arthur Miller, Tennessee Williams, Edward Albee, or Eugene O'Neill, one of the writer's basic preoccupations is the failure of the father and, by implication, the children's avoidance of responsibility. This basic Hamlet-Oedipal situation is evident, I believe, in *Death of a Salesman*, in *Long Day's Journey Into the Night*, and in *The American Dream*; and it is the general situation in *Lie Down in Darkness*. However, Styron enlarges on the drama of family tragedy by strongly implying a sense of personal responsibility to destroy the chain of the past. The creation of a new identity is evident in the characters of his later work. This dynamic destructive-creative resolution is Styron's main preoccupation in *Set This House on Fire* and in *The*

Confessions of Nat Turner, but the static elementary situation exists in *Lie Down in Darkness.*

The inevitable end of Styron's family tragedy clearly shows this intent in the relation between Peyton and Milton Loftis. Just as Milton rationalizes his failures with what Styron terms a "sophomoric fatalism," Peyton challenges her parents directly ("If just she'd had a soul and you'd had some guts" [269]) and again, their generation, the "Lost Generation" ("They weren't lost. What they were doing was losing us" [235]). The one consistent quality in the three Loftises is the failure to assume anything resembling responsibility for their lives. Where many of Faulkner's characters are heavy with guilt, Styron's expend their energies blaming their guilt on someone else (Helen: "God deserted me." [238]). They may feel guilt but never responsibility.

Styron's novel is fatalistic and pointless only in terms of the Loftises. For them, maturity is beyond their reach. But one should not say that Styron is a deterministic writer. At the moment that Milton discovers the edge of the abyss at Peyton's burial, he rubs his eyes Oedipal fashion; and this act represents awareness, a discovery for him. Though there will be no Colonus for Milton, there is one for Styron's other Oedipal heroes. It is their progression beyond self-blindness and despair which Styron traces in his next three novels.

XI "Freud Is Your Bulfinch"

The one consistent feature about practically all the central characters in Styron's novel, one borne out by the actions and the similes which describe them, is that they are dreaming, romantic children. This characteristic is found in several of Styron's early short-story exercises and in *Lie Down in Darkness,* in *The Long March,* and in *Set This House on Fire.* In each instance reality destroys an illusory world and either destroys the characters or forces them to recognition and acceptance. In *Lie Down in Darkness,* the four Loftises, children cut adrift from their past and having no direction to the future, are held together by jealousy, hate, and, possibly, love. For at least one critic, Maxwell Geismar, "the true theme of the novel—all its tenderness and tragedy—lies in the evocation of that childhood world of illusion where all our feelings were direct and open and full and complete." [9] However, the theme of the novel has a wider range than Geismar suggests; for Styron has related the social with the family tragedy. And, if he has evoked the "childhood world of illusion," it is only to indicate the incongruity of clinging to that world when his characters are no longer children.

There is clear evidence in this novel and in Styron's other work of his debt to Freudian psychology; in fact, as we have seen, he thinks that the "new psychiatric wisdom . . . has contributed . . . toward the introspective in fiction." [10] Yet he would, I believe, agree with Nathanael West's judgment about the writer's relation to psychiatry: "Psychology has nothing to do with reality nor should it be used as motivation. The novelist is no longer a psychologist. Psychology can become something much more important. The great body of case histories can be used in the way the ancient writers used their myths. Freud is your Bulfinch; you cannot learn from him." [11]

It is relevant, however, to see that most of Styron's work has its basic psychological roots in the Oedipal situation and that it reflects his need to deal with his own neuroses. "The good writing of any age has always been the product of someone's *neuroses,* and we'd have a mighty dull literature if all the writers that came along were a bunch of happy chuckleheads." [12]

Lie Down in Darkness is a still point from which action begins. In this novel Styron attacks individual and social illusions by presenting them in their falseness and in the evil they generate in the Loftises and their society. Starting from this point, Styron, in *The Long March, Set This House on Fire,* and *The Confessions of Nat Turner,* presents heroes who struggle to liberate themselves from childishness and from a system which keeps them children.

CHAPTER 3

The Rebel Purged:
The Long March

S TYRON'S novella, *The Long March*, published in 1952, has
been singularly neglected by most critics[1] in its significance
to Styron's development and in its thematic parallels to his other
works. Generally regarded as a competent literary exercise, it
has been damned with the faint praise to which Styron has been
occasionally subjected; but, most often, it has been treated as
a single piece.

The novella concerns a thirty-six-mile march ordered by
Colonel Templeton to toughen his regiment of marine reservists
called up during the Korean War. Lieutenant Culver and Captain Mannix both resent the march; but, while Culver chooses
to follow orders, Mannix shows his resentment by driving his
men and by cursing Colonel Templeton for his inhuman command. The plot, which seems like a stock situation in a war
novel, is quite simple; but the poetic metaphors, as in *Lie Down
in Darkness,* enlarge Styron's theme.

If we read the account as a realistic narrative of the conflict
of two wills and if we neglect the essential mood of the novella
which gives it thematic structure, then the plot does resemble
a standard Hollywood product about the marines. Such a reading may lead to a misunderstanding of the story, just as the
misreading of *Lie Down in Darkness* as an exercise in Faulknerian narrative has led to some confusion about that book.
The complexity of the novel lies not in its fairly common subject
but in the poetic description and structural devices which
Styron utilizes in enlarging the narrative into his general theme
of rebellion.

Styron has excellent control over his material, as his technique
with time sequences and framing episodes indicates. Yet, for one
critic, this control makes the novel "a little thematic and abstract." [2] This control affects Styron's characterizations in his

first three novels, and not until Nat Turner does he present a completely successful characterization. But Styron's poetic description and imagery are adequate compensations for his tendency toward abstract characters. Styron's use of nightmare-sharp imagery to describe Culver's feelings as observer-chorus and his use of absurd incidents to motivate Mannix's actions as a rebellious protagonist give the novel its main strength. As for Styron's controlled structure, this technique makes *The Long March* more abstract and didactic than the earlier novel. The central structure of the novel has the marks of classical Greek drama, not only in the allusions to Greek masks, in Mannix's swollen foot, and in Oedipal madness, but in the dramatic control and moral point of acceptance of the human condition. Styron does not praise that condition as much as he speaks for individual survival in a world in which the "centre cannot hold."

The Long March has, therefore, moral implications beyond its contemporary setting. Though Styron is as critical of middle-class intellectual complacency as he is of the dullness of the military mind, he at least grants Culver and Mannix an awareness of their situation and a sense of their humanity in the face of fate or necessity. Thematically, *The Long March* marks Styron's movement from the tragic hopelessness of *Lie Down in Darkness* to the affirmation of existence by survival in *Set This House on Fire* and in *The Confessions of Nat Turner*.

I "The Rebellious Soul" and the "System"

The novella is divided into five sections built around the framework of a forced march in a Carolina marine camp at the time of the Korean War; and the central characters, Mannix and Culver, are World War II reservists who have been called from their illusory peacetime into an illusory war. The contemporary cold war background reflects man's general sense of ineffectuality in controlling his destiny, and it is also related to Styron's general theme that Americans must forego the dream of childhood, stop mourning the loss of innocence, and begin to examine the world their naïveté has in part created. In an article about his tribulations in adapting the novella for television, Styron describes his story:

The Rebel Purged: The Long March

My story's hero is also a rebellious soul, a young Marine reserve officer whose mutinous rage against authority in general, and his commanding officer in particular, leads to his downfall. . . . He resists the System and it is his ruin. You cannot buck the System—I think that is what I was trying to say—for if you do you will pull disaster down upon your head. . . . At the end of my story the captain (who is not without his foolish and impulsive moments), having faced down his commanding officer at the conclusion of a senseless and brutal hike ordered by the same CO, stands ready to receive a court martial. The tragedy is implicit here.[3]

In the novella, Styron neither damns nor praises the "System" particularly; he indicates the futility of rebellion without a cause. Ironically, in the course of his rebellion, *because of its pointlessness,* Mannix adapts the clichés and forms of the "System" in order to oppose it. This psychological subtlety in the novella, as much as Styron's descriptions, makes it a work of art.

Disturbed over the mishandling of his book by television writers, Styron wrote that "Divorced of its philosophical content, the narrative becomes utterly routine" and that the scriptwriters misconceived matters by the reduction of "my bedevilled, desperate captain" to a "self-pitying hero" who, far from eliciting the viewer's sympathies, deserves to be punished. At least one critic, who regards the unsympathetic attitude toward Mannix as the correct one, speaks of Styron's concept of the Marine Corps as a "kind of monastic order united in love, symbolized by the ritual which must be entered into unquestionably, with complete obedience." [4] Despite the excellent analysis of Styron's metaphors by this critic, we find little or no support for his view that Styron intended to do more than present the Marines as a system—as a "collection of attitudes," not human but mechanical ones. The humanity is found in Culver and Mannix, the observer and protagonist, respectively, of a drama of rebellion.

II Technique: Contrast and Metaphor

A close examination of Styron's techniques, his use of allusive description and economy of language, demonstrates the controlled force of the novella. The narrative opens with a scene of surrealistic horror in which the eight dead marines lie "as if sprayed from a hose, they were shreds of bone, gut and dangling tissue" (3);[5] and their surviving companions moan in pain. This central image of human parts scattered among inanimate objects ("slick nude litter of intestine and shattered blue bones, among which forks and spoons peeked out like so many pathetic metal flowers" [6]) is reworked in varied forms throughout the novel. At this point, it underscores the feelings of Lieutenant Culver who has been called back from a dream of freedom and security to the reality of contemporary existence; and it is his resentment which provides the initial consciousness of the story.

Later, the image emphasizes the thematic conflict in the novella between the mechanical coldness of Colonel Templeton and the tragic humanity of Captain Mannix. But, originally, the slaughter of the innocent soldiers clearly symbolizes the shattered sense of order in Culver's life. This sense of order is recalled through another recurring image which is juxtaposed with the scene of a winter afternoon—a Sunday stroll in which "pink-cheeked and contented" persons remain undisturbed by "crimson alarms" of headlines. Eighteenth-century music—Bach, Mozart, or Haydn—gives Culver a sense of order through which he transcends to another and happier sphere of childhood.

If we look at the first few pages of Styron's original manuscript,[6] we find that he made a conscious effort to maintain two views of the scene: a straight naturalistic description and Culver's view. After the initial description, Styron established Culver as a focal consciousness, an observer, who in turn is observed by the reader. Though Styron described Culver's civilian life with its security and routine in sharp, distinct detail, he cut sharply into a later description of Culver's earlier experiences around the marine camp. This description would have taken the reader back to an even remoter period from the present action and would have reduced the effect of Styron's narrative. It was most important for Styron to establish the contrast between the apparent harmony of civilian life for Culver and the chaos and disorder of the present. In these first few pages, we observe also Styron's choice of words and his avoidance of awkward phrasing: "hose" replaces "flit-gun," and "blood and brain" are juxtaposed not with "pork-chops" but with "scattered mess-kits" to give the mechanistic-human contrast.

Styron pointedly contrasts this world of logic, peace, and order to the chaos of wartime life in a strange land of tourist cabins and "unlovely mementoes." His technique in this first section is to shift from the explosion as a "crazy, insulting impact at Culver's belly" (6) to his protest at the explosion which blew up his private world, to a speculation of the illusory order, and, finally, to the chaos of war. Thus, Styron creates with skill and economy the ambiance for his novel by following the natural thought of his observer, Culver.

III Immediacy of Effect: Technique and Characterization as Theme

Styron's main theme about the shattering effects of existence and reality is developed as it was in *Lie Down in Darkness* through a series of moments which develop his narrative before the actual march begins. For example, the second section returns to the sound of the explosion, reworking the image "scattered faces peering toward the noise, their knives and forks suspended" (12), to bring Culver and the reader back to the reality of the moment. Styron then rapidly delineates the two major characters, Colonel Templeton and Captain Mannix, and the officers and men who assume varied stances in relation to the two apparently opposing points of view.

Colonel Templeton fulfills the role of a priest of war who dogmatically does his duty; a man unreasoningly in the grip of an idea, he gives little sign of humanity toward others since he has surrendered it to the marines. Indeed, he is Styron's most adamantine character. Since this work is a novella, Styron cannot develop Templeton's character as he does Helen Loftis's in *Lie Down in Darkness* or Mason Flagg's in *Set This House on Fire;* but Templeton resembles them: he is the embodiment of all the values of his community or group.

Styron's metaphors of this effeminate actor-priest suggest a comparison with Norman Mailer's General Cummings in *The Naked and the Dead*. In Mailer's novel, the fully developed characterization of a sick military mind who has an aptitude for power, the "only hunger which has meaning" for Cummings, is demonstrably pure illusion since he, like all authoritarians, is as subject to whim and chance as he is to the stratagems of his enemies. The conclusion of *The Naked and the Dead,* in which the island is captured in a few days by blunder rather than by strategy, underscores the absurdity of Cummings's "power." In Styron's novella, however, Colonel Templeton remains an impassive, unthinking automaton who barely shows any emotion or desire and who has absolutely no human connections—not even the perverted relations of Mailer's general. Templeton, who is always being observed by Culver, first appears as an ecclesiastic, "Prematurely aged and perhaps even wise" (18), then as a ham actor who "was not himself evil or unjust" (30), or again as a person of "priestlike, religious fervor . . . devout but inclined toward mercy" (30).

Culver's early view of the Colonel's "act" as that of a rigid military type and as one that is, therefore, "less offensive, less imperious than it might be," is carried through the narrative not as a defense but as a statement of fact. For the Colonel at the end is hardly a man but is a collection of attitudes. Elsewhere, Styron has described the professional military man as unconcerned with patriotism. "His devotion is to a service not to a country"; and, says Styron, "A true military man is a mercenary . . . and it is within the world of soldiering that he finds his only home." [7] The most chilling aspect of the Colonel is his utter lack of humanity, of good or evil; for he is a mechanical toy whose reaction to Mannix's challenge is the stereotype of the Western hero who reaches for his gun. That Culver loathes rather than hates the Colonel because he is nonhuman is apparent from the way he regards the Colonel's concern for Mannix's wound: "He didn't hate him for himself, nor even for his brutal march. Bad as it was, there were no doubt worse ordeals; it was at least a peaceful landscape they had to cross. But he did hate him for his perverse and brainless gesture: squatting in the sand, gently, almost indecently now, stroking Mannix's foot, he had too long been conditioned by the system to perform with grace a human act" (89).

In an early scene Styron appears to have set Mannix and the Colonel as contrasts of human victim and inhuman torturer, respectively. But the confrontation is deceptive, for Styron subtly draws a number of comparative scenes between the two which suggest greater similarities than differences. Certainly, they are unlike physically; the Colonel's small hands and pretty face are markedly different from Mannix's huge, hairy frame. Mannix detests the Colonel as a symbol of "absolute and unquestioned authority." But, as they face each other in the tent after the Colonel has announced the march, Culver sees them as strangely similar: "In the morbid, comfortless light they were like classical Greek masks, made of chrome or tin, reflecting an almost theatrical disharmony; the Colonel's fleeting grin sculpted cleanly and prettily in the unshadowed air above the Captain's darkened, downcast face where, for a flicker of a second, something outraged and agonized was swiftly graven and swiftly scratched out" (29).

The Colonel's face is fixed with the certitude, the equilibrium of the dogmatist who never doubts his actions, while, for an instant, the beginnings of Mannix's terrible anger are part of his mask. Styron creates the tension of their struggle by present-both men in terms of their inflexible masks. For Mannix loses his identity as surely as the Colonel. He discards his humanity, not unlike a minor Ahab; and, because of his monomaniacal hatred of the Colonel, he blinds himself to his own and to his men's suffering. However, by the end of the novel he has regained his humanity and has even given Culver a renewed sense of values. Minor characters such as Major Lawrence, a boot-licking "spoiled and arrogant baby of five" with cheeks of "peacetime fleshiness," and O'Leary, whose dedication is of a more acceptable, oxlike variety, are worthy of the Colonel's indulgence because of their loyalty; both serve as contrasts to Mannix rebellious mood.

Additional background is supplied by Culver's drowsing dream in which he recalls Mannix's challenge and the Colonel's defense of the march. When Mannix first speaks to Culver, his "unqualified cynicism" is offset by his comic exasperation with the Colonel; but his bitter comments ultimately generate fears in Culver. There is logic in Mannix's point that a thirty-six-mile forced march without some shorter conditioning hikes is absurd, but there never seems to be any question of Mannix's "making it." The fear is Culver's, and his anxiety about the march becomes symbolic to him of the terrible load of his loneliness and isolation. Listening to Mannix renews Culver's earlier anxieties; he feels "adrift at sea . . . ignorant of any direction or of any points of the globe" (34). He feels profoundly alone with his nameless anxiety, for the world of order is stripped away.

The pointless maneuvers, the constant movement, and the lack of sleep have disoriented time and space. The sun's blinding heat and light make the day a continual inferno; the night offers no respite; and Culver experiences the feeling of death while still subject to the terrors of life. Culver's mind is obsessed with the march and with his fear of failure. This fear is amplified after Mannix lumbers to bed while Culver sits in the "chill and cramped universe of the tent" (40) and listens to the wailing signals of the radio. His own messages in absurd code make him feel childish, and he empathizes completely with Mannix's feelings of helplessness. Yet Culver, like Loftis and later Peter Leverett in *Set This House on Fire*, cannot bring himself to act— not even to offset his frustration.

IV Mannix's Rebellion: Cause and Effect

Culver's speculations about Mannix as hero relate directly to Styron's idea of the equivalent blindness of the dogmatist and the heretic. Mannix's scarred body testifies that he has suffered as a hero, but his experiences have been absurd, not heroic. Indeed, Styron frames Mannix's brave, perilous, and rocklike rebellion with two significant episodes pertinent to the nature of his rebellion. In the first scene, Mannix yells for help into a broken telephone while being shelled by his own men; in the second, he faces death while being held outside a window by two drunken marines. Interspersed with these two episodes are a series of incidents in which Mannix rebels against the dehumanizing abstraction that is the Marine Corps. His muttering during the cliché-filled lecture and his "manifesto" that the reserves "should be home with their families" is controlled, but his passionate feeling comes through. "His words had the quality, the sternness, of an absolute and unequivocal fact, as if they had been some intercession for grace spoken across the heads of a courtroom by a lawyer so quietly convinced of his man's innocence that there was no need for gesticulations or frenzy" (51).

Mannix thus becomes as dogmatic and as blind as his antagonist, the Marine Corps; and his rebellion is based on self-pity and personal pride. This situation is distinctly different from the two earlier ones in which Mannix had no self-pity or pride but was trying to survive. Culver sees him "projected against Heaven's Gate" (52), the officers' club, at which Mannix beweeps his "outcast state" and troubles "deaf heaven" with his "bootless cries." The background to Mannix's voice is supplied by the distant bleating saxophone, "indecisive and sad, like the nation and the suffocating summer, neither at peace or at war" (55); and the pointlessness of individual protest appears to Culver to be more dangerous than absurd. The danger becomes more evident when later in the novel we see Mannix brutalized by the "System." Before his redemption at the end of the novel, Mannix must be purged of that element of the "System" within himself.

The image of Mannix, clutching the air as he hangs high over the street while his legs slowly slip in the wet hands of the two marines, is a foretaste of the novella's end. When the moment or recollection of terror and helplessness is over, Mannix laughs listlessly; and Culver sees his bitterness melt: "he seemed no longer the man who could sicken himself with resentment, but relaxed, pliable even, like a huge hairy baby soothed by the wash of elemental tides, ready to receive anything, all, into that great void in his soul which bitterness and rebellion had briefly left vacant—all—the finality of more suffering, or even death" (59). This view of Mannix is almost identical, even to physical description, with our final view of him at the end of the novella. Through this repetition of description Styron connects the early scene with Mannix's return from insanity.

V   Order Exploded: The March Begins

At this point in the novel, however, Culver knows only the fear, uncertainty, and loneliness which Mannix's "resigned silence" feeds. The children on the lawn and the ordered music are lost in the chaos of his present life. At this moment, Culver, who is wakened by the noonday light, returns again to the moment of explosion, which tears into Culver's consciousness, thrusting him "back into the blinding sun, the meaningless scenery of a fantastic noon." The larger frame which encompasses its one and two is that of the explosion scene and, with it, the horror of the young marine, his face blasted away, his head surrounded by darting insects. The explosion releases Mannix's hatred; his calmness, serenity, and humor fail him; and he becomes a furious man who blinded by his rage, cries, "Won't they ever let us alone?" (63-64).

The third and fourth sections deal with the march and with Mannix's self-imposed agony when he accepts, for example, the nail in his shoe as part of his bitter fortune. Culver realizes that the explosion had left Mannix's "raw nerves exposed" and that his loss of humanity is clear not only from his lack of concern for himself but also from his bullying attitude toward his men. Throughout the march Mannix, who appears demented, loses himself in his madness as thoroughly as the Colonel does in his coolness. Pitted against such an enemy, Mannix accepts the Colonel's "challenge" as personal and answers it with his masochistic pride.

With the "bloody wasteland" as a setting and with the "brainless chorale" of frogs emanating from the swamp, the marines begin their march. Mannix's strident commands are to Culver those of a "fanatic with one idea: to last" and to spite the Colonel. Mannix's moods range from mania to depressed silences; he viciously abuses his men; and his irrationality leads to imaginary conversations with the Colonel on whom he has centered all the hatred and frustration of his rebellion. Culver, on the other hand, hopes for relief from the Colonel, whom he has hitherto regarded as a stern but merciful father. Neither Mannix nor Culver receives the desired response of wrath or mercy, for the Colonel continues relentlessly. When the Colonel stops to examine Mannix's wound, Culver sees Templeton's total lack of humanity. Culver then realizes that Templeton is as indifferent as the universe to man's pain. While this moment is one of revelation to Culver, it is the moment of battle for Mannix, who challenges the Colonel; the lack of Templeton's response only infuriates Mannix further.

The march continues; and, as dawn breaks, the lash of Mannix's voice driving his exhausted men on seems to Culver the one continuing impression of the chaotic night. Styron's description of the "almost prehistoric sun" recalls the vision of the shattered dead, the explosion which blots from Culver's memory any consoling scenes of his past. As Culver's mind slips in fevered blankness, he becomes deranged in the heat; and, brief space, he loses connection with reality: not stopping to help a sick marine, passing through a crowd of butterflies, being taunted by passing marines in a jeep, and finally seeing a scarlet tanager metamorphose into "eight butchered corpses."

VI "Rebellion in Reverse"

Winding his watch brings Culver back to time and to a scene of Mannix's bullying. He intervenes, appealing to Mannix's humanity. Until this point, Mannix has been speaking to his men in the brutal clichés of the march; but, when Culver pleads with him, Mannix becomes inarticulate and turns away in bitter isolation. Determined to prove himself beyond the bounds of sanity, and with his men in bondage to his madness, Mannix has lost all sense of proportion on hearing that the Colonel may have quit. Mannix has become a fanatic prophet, a Moses, who whips his followers under the burning sun.

Culver realizes that Mannix and he have never escaped being "marines"—"The corruption begun years ago in his drill-field feet had climbed up, overtaken him and had begun to rot his brain." Paradoxically, Mannix wishes to prove this corps "esprit" to the Colonel. Maxwell Geismar, who refers to the captain as "Nixman," points out that Mannix's "form of rebellion is indeed simply to outdo his fantastic Colonel's wildest notions of a Marine." [8] By the end of the novel, Mannix is cured of his monomania—his "rebellion in reverse."

As Mannix gathers the last of his men to be marched, out of pride and spite, for the last six miles, he faces the Colonel: Mannix was no longer a simple doubter but the heretic, and was about to receive judgment" (109). As they confront each other, they are "twin profiles"; for each has surrendered his identity: one, to the marine "system"; the other, to sightless rage; and both men lack Culver's compassion. The Colonel's gesture of power reveals the pointlessness of Mannix's "rebellion in reverse," for Mannix's Oedipal blindness has had no more point to it than the Colonel's command to make the march. The absurdity is underscored by the description of Mannix's face as he completes the march: "it was the painted, suffering face of a clown."

VII The Observer Reflects: The Rebel Endures

At the end, Culver, unable to rest, reviews the incidents of the march and of the explosion against the setting of "Heaven's Gate." Thinking of the eight dead boys, who are now past caring and who were ignorant of what their life and death meant, Culver recalls the softness of Emily Dickinson's "Safe in their alabaster chambers . . . sleep the meek members of the resurrection." The image of the boys, which carried with it the explosion symbolizing the destruction of Culver's ordered life, now calls up a mature acceptance of real tragedy and, with it, comes the "tender miracle of pity." Culver feels a "deep vast hunger" for the peace which had always escaped him. When he considers the significance of the march, Culver can no more hate the Colonel than before; but he now recognizes him for what he is: "hardly a man at all, but just a quantity of attitudes . . . remote from Culver's world" (117). Culver's recognition is a significant change; for, like the hero of Stephen Crane's *Red Badge of Courage*, he recognizes how disproportionate were his fears.

Mannix, the tragic-absurd hero, summons a more despairing picture to Culver, whose sympathy for Mannix increases after his "defeat" by the Colonel. Paradoxically, the Colonel's "victory" reduces Mannix to nothing less than a *true* man, and he emerges as more of a human being than the Colonel. Styron draws a final picture of suffering man when Mannix, with "taut drawn-down mouth . . . of tortured and gigantic suffering" (119), faces the Negro maid who speaks sympathetically to him: "Culver would remember this: the two of them communicating across that chasm one unspoken moment of sympathy and understanding" (119-20). For Culver, the sensitive observer, renders Mannix's redemptive act as meaningful.[9] We see Mannix again as a man of flesh and bone; scarred and naked as Odysseus on the Phaeacian shore, he appears as possessed "not with self-pity but only with the tone of a man" who has endured and lasted. Mannix's madness is over and he is reborn through the purgatory of suffering to become a man "too weary to tell . . . anything but what was true" (120).

Styron, who originally thought of entitling the story "A Walk Through the Night," obviously felt that "The Long March" was a better title for the implications of his story. The march brings out Mannix's rebellion against the "System" and the need to assert his own being. David Galloway [10] has made an excellent case for Mannix as a rebel in Camus's sense of the word. Yet it is as important to see that Styron's interest in the rebel and in the idea of rebellion is twofold: personal and social. Primarily for Styron the great value of action is that, through rebellion, the rebel discovers the evils of the "System" in himself, cuts through his self-illusions, and exorcises his devils to become a mature person. This idea is further developed in Cass in *Set This House on Fire* and in Nat in *The Confessions of Nat Turner*. Camus may have given Styron his rebel in an ideological sense, but psychological analysis gives the American novelist his direction and theme: the emergence of maturity.

It was to be eight years before Styron's next novel, *Set This House on Fire*, but the similar moral concerns and themes of choice and freedom are present there in contradistinction to the fatalistic world of *Lie Down in Darkness*. *The Long March* is the first of Styron's clear-cut novels of rebellion, which were to culminate in the figure of Nat Turner.

CHAPTER 4

Rebellion of Wrath and Laughter:
Set This House on Fire

WILLIAM STYRON's second full-length novel, *Set This House on Fire*, was long in appearing; but it was expectantly awaited by critics and by the reading public. The result of Styron's labors, his purpose in the novel, and his success have been evaluated, examined, and re-examined until by now the significance of the novel has almost been buried by criticism of it. The reason for greater critical attention to *Set This House on Fire* than to *Lie Down in Darkness* is quite transparent when we consider the range of contemporary criticism. In describing in *Set This House on Fire* Cass Kinsolving's struggle to free himself, Styron provides enough symbolism and myth to satisfy the formalists; he sufficiently discusses the malaise of American society to appeal to sociologists and European critics; he sufficiently suggests the influence of Camus and possibly Kierkegaard to interest Existentialists;[1] and he manages to attract the attention of sundry critics who have been intrigued by what they have considered to be Styron's flamboyant failures in style and in structure.

Whatever the critics' interest, the novel represents a basic contest between two related attitudes. The first of these is caricatured in the artist Cass Kinsolving who is the sum of all the flaws of men living in a Romantic-Puritan society (self-indulgence, self-pity, guilt obsession) but who is marked as a rebel by his urgent discontent. Hyperbole in deed and word is his medium. The second caricature is Mason Flagg, a monstrous extension of the hero and a personification of all the defects of an antihuman society. The contest takes place within a Gothic nightmare of brutal violence, and the result is a combination of satire and the tale of horror.[2] There is the observer-chorus as well in the character of Peter Leverett who moves from a dull awareness and self-consciousness to a greater sensibility by observing and commenting on the actions of the two other main characters. *Set This House on Fire* is a novel of revolt like Styron's other novels, as we have seen. Indeed in referring to his latest work, Styron has said, "I realized all my work is predicated on revolt in one way or another." [3]

I A Gothic Satire

In Styron's fiction, the journeys of his rebellious protagonists pass through the apocalyptic vision of the American nightmare. The distortions of the dream, the infernal lens through which his characters view their reality, are grotesque parodies of the superficial reality of the American dream. In *Set This House on Fire,* Styron employs this technique continually; the result is a Gothic tale in which the grotesque is used for moral and satiric effect. [4]

Coincident with the appearance of *Set This House on Fire* was the publication of Leslie Fiedler's *Love and Death in the American Novel* in 1960; and, interestingly enough, Styron's novel fulfills Fiedler's prescription for the Gothic fiction which can best express an American nightmare. For we find in the novel the superreal, grotesque characters, even the exotic and Gothic setting, and the incidents of sexual and fatal violence joined with the moral struggle of Cass Kinsolving to free himself from his masochistic guilt. Fiedler reminds us that Melville, Hawthorne, Twain, and Faulkner satisfy "the dimly perceived need of many Americans to have their national existence projected in terms of a pact with the devil. . . . There is scarcely a heroic ideal of our native life which is not, in one or another of these writers' gothic books, illuminated by a weird and lurid light. Such ideals are not . . . merely travestied and debunked . . . [but are] raised to a tragic power." [5] To me, Styron is not so much concerned with the tragic consequences of such a pact in *Set This House on Fire* as he is involved in Cass Kinsolving's struggle to exorcise those defects of the society in himself. In the process, the values of his society are satirized and vilified along with the Romantic Puritanism which binds Cass.

Cass Kinsolving, a preposterous character, is not only hyperbolic and bombastic in his speech but is also human and absurd in his actions. Despite his irritating vacillation between self-indulgence and self-flagellation, he, like Mannix in *The Long March*, is sympathetically characterized. He has an energy and spirit which, by contrast, make all the other characters listless. But his struggle, though ending on a comparatively subdued note, has that sense of apocalypse which pervades all of Styron's fiction. R. W. B. Lewis in his essay "Days of Wrath and Laughter," speaks, while not mentioning Styron, of the current "imagery of disaster" to which has been added the "pervasive sense of the preposterous":

The addition may be all important. It testifies, anyhow, to the healthful influence of Nathanael West; for it was West, following hard on Melville and Mark Twain, who established for contemporary American writing the vision of the ludicrous catastrophe, and who searched out and bodied forth some of its human sources. A complex apocalyptic vision ran through all of West's short novels; but it reached its climax, of course, in the last book he lived to write. *The Day of the Locust* (1939) borrowed its title and much of its conviction about the course of human events from the seminal Book of the Apocalypse, or Revelations, in the New Testament. . . . It has been by exploiting a perspective of just that kind that novelists as variously gifted as Ralph Ellison and John Barth and Joseph Heller and Thomas Pynchon have made the day of doom the great saturnalia of our time—a *dies irae* converted into a *dies irae risusque*. For our literature and our spiritual history are in fact caught between the wrath and the laughter; and our survival, in many meanings of the word, may hang upon the outcome.[6]

Styron has written praisefully of West's novel;[7] and his specific interest in Twain and his belief in satire as a means of articulating man's dilemmas indicate his preoccupation with this technique. Styron's use of satire in language and situation becomes even more obvious when we examine the Gothic elements in *Set This House on Fire*.

Recounted through the memories of Cass Kinsolving, a painter, and Peter Leverett, a lawyer, *Set This House on Fire* is a comic American Gothic fable. A psychologically blocked and alcoholic painter, Cass appears to be trapped by his extravagant patron, Mason Flagg, into being one of his corrupted sycophants. Believing that Flagg had raped and killed Francesca, a young Italian girl, Cass kills him only to discover that Mason had not killed her. Cass's murder of Mason becomes a ritual act, an exorcism of the childlike devil of a corrupted society. Though Cass's crime is known by a local policeman, he is permitted to return to America, free of the evil which had possessed him. These are the surface details of the plot, but the nature of Styron's narration and the revelation of Cass's character give the novel a significance that, like Dostoevski's *The Brothers Karamazov*, goes far beyond the limits of a Gothic mystery.

In Styron's Gothic world, like that of Nathanael West, forms and shapes are grotesquely presented; and the sense of proportion and order necessary to a classical Sophoclean tragic view is clearly lacking.[8] In this respect, *Set This House on Fire* is too hallucinatory and surreal in its violence and too ambiguous in its resolution to be tragic. Basically, the problem of interpretation rests in examining the two perspectives of Peter and Cass and in remembering *not* to identify Styron's view exactly with that of one or the other character. Both characters are Gullivers in that their vision is distorted: in Peter's case, by his own inadequacy and mediocrity; in Cass's, by his crippling sense of guilt and frustration. Their reflections about the events at Sambuco years later are an attempt to bring both the characters and the theme into focus by the end of the novel.

II The Italian Setting

Setting is pertinent to Styron's theme at the inception of *Set This House on Fire,* for his Italian landscape is particularly appropriate in the narration of a Gothic-grotesque novel. Nathalia Wright, in *American Novelists in Italy,* makes a number of interesting speculations about American writers in Italy. She sees contemporary writers as using the Italian moral and physical setting as a place of self-discovery for their American characters, much as nineteenth-century American novelists (Cooper, Hawthorne, Howells, and James) did. Though her main interest is in nineteenth-century writers, she observes that in both earlier and contemporary writers "The characters which they portray often seem to be in search of something, and often acquire in Italy a sense of direction or a feeling of human brotherhood." [9]

Italy represents, therefore, a moral experience not available in America. Hawthorne, for instance, combined Gothic elements with moral symbolism in his romance, *The Marble Faun;* for Cooper, in *The Water Witch,* the Italian way of life appears more attractive than the provinciality and commercialism of the Americans; and James and Howells both use the Italian moral viewpoint in contrast to the often dangerous naïveté of Americans. Styron adds the new and disturbing element of the corrupting influence of America in Europe, and he draws corollaries between the life of the miserable poor in Italy and that of the black men in America.

In an excellent essay, "Adjustment, Tragic Humanism, and Italy," [10] which contains a detailed discussion of Styron's *Set This House on Fire,* Arthur Winner regards Styron's novel with its balance of Gothic and Arcadian aspects as a background for a struggle between innocence and evil as a notable example of the use of the Italian setting. His descriptions of Rome, Sambuco, and the Tramonti Valley tie in directly with his apparent desire to write a Gothic moral tale in which the double American evils of Romantic naïveté and corrupting affluence are exorcised by the artist-hero. Cass—influenced by the scenes around him and troubled by the rationalistic arguments of the policeman, Luigi—slowly realizes his limits and his powers.

III   The Three Main Characters: Peter Rabbit

The novel opens with a description from a travel guide, an apparently objective account of the beautiful landscape and romantic ancient ruins of Sambuco. The "objective" tone, however, is the cool, detached voice of Peter Leverett who first describes himself and then Cass Kinsolving, the true protagonist of the novel. Peter Leverett observes the contest between Cass Kinsolving and Mason Flagg apparently without recognizing what a number of Styron's many commentators have seen: the moral significance of the struggle of the artist to free himself from the claims of the affluent, antihuman society.[11] Leverett, whose moral and intellectual outlook is that of his illustrious namesake, Peter Rabbit, tells us that, although he is a "realist" who makes the "pleasant best" of his destiny, he is subject to disturbing dreams and to personal guilt about Flagg's death, the central incident in the novel. His curiosity about the murder and the events of Sambuco is based on a sense that they are important, but we never feel that he really comprehends what has taken place.

Peter, whose strong resemblance to Nick Carroway in Fitzgerald's *Great Gatsby* fades as Styron's novel continues, is destined to be "borne back ceaselessly into the past." His nostalgia and bourgeois Romanticism inhibit his development toward awareness. In contrast, Cass's response is that of a man who has found some direction in life by confronting reality, by knowing his limits, and by re-creating himself from his struggle. We expect that, for Peter, the revelation of the Sambuco experience will in some way parallel the awakening of Cass Kinsolving to reality. However, much as Peter is moved by his father's diatribe at the beginning of the novel, his general diffidence toward the nightmarish quality of American life and his avoidance of any relationship which might do more than superficially brush against his self-centered shell characterize him as a person who fears reality. Peter even regards himself as a fixed set of mediocre, bourgeois, and sentimental responses. Confrontation with reality never gives Peter much more than a vague sense of nostalgia and ennui—never a plausible despair. He remains remarkably untouched by events throughout the novel, and even his "commitment" to the young lady at the very end is not very convincing.

Peter's counterfeit spiritual metamorphosis begins with his account of his self-pitying mood and his isolation on his way to Sambuco. All the horror and grotesqueness which mark most of the events in the novel begin slowly during Leverett's Dantesque journey to the South. At the start, his journey is uneventful; he reluctantly leaves Rome with its tattered Ava Gardner posters. Although he senses a lull before a "decisive instant," he remains, in true Leverett fashion, "unstirred." His night journey gives him at first a sense of liberation and, then, as he turns to the Campania, one of isolation; the music of Beethoven fades on the radio to be replaced by the Hillbilly Gasthaus; and a feeling of complete exhaustion strikes him. All that follows appears as if it were part of Peter's grotesque dream. As if he were entering a dream world, Peter stops; and, symptomatic of his general withdrawal from reality, he seals himself in his car. Yet his dreams are "exhausting nightmares" interlaced with "breaths out of time past," the fantastic grounded in the actual.

The description of the Italian landscape, the "devil's pageant" of cars, the heat rising in "greasy waves," and withal the gradual increase in tension in Peter are other examples of Styron's apocalyptic vision at work. The accident with Lucano Di Lieto (Light of Joy), a man who courts disaster as extravagantly as Peter avoids it, links Di Lieto with Peter and later with Cass. (Di Lieto, who remains in a coma until the end of the novel, revives at approximately the same time that Cass emerges from his self-conscious coma of insensitivity.) For Di Lieto, until the accident, is, like most of the other Italians in the novel, a "survivor"; he is a man who asserts his existence against nothingness, just as Cass does at the novel's end.

Again, in the epilogue of the novel, there is a letter from a nun to Peter telling of Di Lieto's recovery: he is "like the Phoenix risen from the ashes of his own affliction," a clear parallel to Cass's emergence. The accident at the end of Peter's nightmare journey brings him directly into the circle, the moral focus of responsibility. But Peter, himself, remains virtually unaffected; and he forms a distinct contrast to Cass's self-discovery. Peter has a degree of perception but no real self-awareness. Inhibited, rabbit-like, he is in awe of Mason's supposed amoral sexual freedom and of Mason's wealth. In fact, he reveals himself most obviously in his relationship to Flagg.

IV   Mason Flagg: The Bourgeois Dream

Mason represents the American bourgeois dream come true. He operates on a grand, although ungenerous, scale, producing a motion picture about the Cenci (a farce in modern dress); and he is surrounded by all the superficial types recognizable to viewers of Fellini's films. Peter is the anxious bourgeois observer who is destined to be hypnotized by Flagg's false freedom and who is unable to understand, except in the vaguest way, Cass's madness. Essentially an observer, Peter finds it simpler to be amazed by Flagg's flamboyance than to be affected by Cass's struggle.

Reasonable, cautious, a man who changes only slightly in comparison to the angry or passionate man, and whose major justification is that of a slightly uncomfortable foil to Cass, Peter is vicariously thrilled by Mason's amoral fireworks at prep school, by his Oedipal relationship with his Wendy (Peter Pan) mother, and by his pseudocreative life as a Hollywood producer. Peter explains his feelings about Mason and the power and freedom he represents: "Being a fairly inward-looking person, and one carefully attuned to the psychiatric overtones in this age, I have often wondered whether there was not something homosexual in our connection in my attraction to Mason. . . . I think I simply felt when I was near him that he was more imaginative, more intelligent than I, and at the same time more corrupt (more corrupt, that is, than I could allow myself to be, as much as I tried) . . ." (136).

This aspect of Peter's relationship is central to an understanding of Styron's theme. Peter, despite his occasional discernment, is wholly preoccupied with Flagg as a symbol of freedom. Cyril Arnovan in his article "Les romans de William Styron, sees as the essential point of the book "the enchantment an average man feels vis-à-vis a millionaire," and Mason is the incarnation of that aspect of American life to Peter.[12]

Mason Flagg is much closer to being a caricature than a character in the novel. Cass refers to him as a "monster," an epithet Milton Loftis had cast at Helen; for Mason is the embodiment of the worst aspects of the spoiled-society child of contemporary America: insensitive, boorish, arrogant, pseudointellectual, pseudoartistic, and power hungry. In the scenes at Sambuco, which are based on Styron's brief sojourn with the Hollywood company making *Beat the Devil* in 1953 at Rapallo, we are introduced to a Mason Flagg as seen through Peter's bewildered eyes. Flagg appears as the great man, as garrulous, as waving goodbye to his last writer, as carrying on about Italian women, and, in general, as playing the role of the prep-school marvel around Peter. Peter soon discovers the phony and superficial nature of the production and the evil way in which Flagg controls the people about him; but he remains because he is fascinated by Flagg's pyrotechnical display.

The hotel with its effeminate proprietor, Windgasser; the mixed atmosphere of Edwardian decadence; and the memories of the 1920's do not repel Peter. If anything, the atmosphere spurs him into a nostalgic reverie of Mason, the lost boy, and Wendy, his mother. In his reminiscence, Peter is drawn to Mason even when the other boys at school are disillusioned with him, even when he has been proven a liar. Because of Peter's own subdued and austere life, he is impressed by Mason's alternating coldness and semi-incestuous relationship with Wendy. That Mason continues this Oedipal role with his mistress, Rosemarie, is all too obvious. She not only resembles his mother but holds the same intellectual outlook of "conventional morals and monied security" (94) and a similar belief that Gibran's *The Prophet* is great poetry.

Mason's superficial views about either art or human relationships shift and change with fashion, but they have the one consistency of being totally antihumanistic and anti-intellectual: "Art is dead . . . Science is the new Muse. . . . Couple science with a general leveling of taste everywhere, and the demise is inevitable. . . . By the end of the century art—painting, music, poetry, drama—all of them, they'll be as dead as the labyrinthodont" (145-46). Again, " 'Sex is the last frontier,' he was saying somewhere behind me. 'In art as in life, Peter, sex is the only area left where men can find full expression of their individuality, full freedom. Where men cast off the constrictions and conventions of society and regain their identity as humans. . . . I mean the total exploration of sex, as Sade envisioned it. . . . It's what you might call *le nouveau libertinage*' " (151).

Though Mason speaks of human identity, his actions toward himself and others (particularly toward his wives and Francesca) are still those of the self-gratifying child who is completely insensitive to others. He is sterile physically as well as artistically, and practically all his sexual actions require public attendance or participation. The inadequacies which lead him to tell fantastic stories about his wartime deeds are also part of Mason's own psychological drama of substitution. Moreover, he uses creative people to give himself an aura of creativity. But, in truth, Mason is ineffectual. Even his control over Cass is illusory, for Cass recognizes what Mason is shortly after their first meeting. In the detailed comic description at which Cass excels, he recounts that Flagg believed him to be another and far more successful painter. When he had shown Flagg some poor sketches, he had praised them highly. But to Cass, involved in his failures as a human being, the paintings are "fidgety, selfish little corners of some private view, a bunch of aborted, stunted notions wriggling in a vacuum" (386).

Cass's remarks about his own paintings indicate a recognition of his sickness and of his having been his own prisoner. Cass understands quite clearly that he holds himself in bondage and that he has to be free, not from Flagg, but from himself; but he does not have the ability to change himself. Flagg, who is most distasteful to Cass, is the very embodiment of what Cass hates in himself: willfulness, self-indulgence, insensitivity, and childishness. Flagg also represents America, and his rape of Francesca and his domination of Cass are the actions which compel Cass to murder Flagg: " 'Mason,' he said slowly, 'Uncle Sugar.' I got so that with Mason I was as helpless as Romulus, sucking on the fat tit of a wolf. But this day here, this day he gave me that bottle, I had no idea how far *in* I would get with Mason, how deep and involved. Any more than I had the notion that in another way I'd rouse myself—God knows how I did it—and grasp a truth about the shabby and contorted life I'd been leading and make at least a stab at salvaging something out of the wreckage . . .' " (402).

V Mason's People

Peter regards the persons in Mason's group much as Styron observed the guests at Peyton's wedding in *Lie Down in Darkness*. The characters of Mason's group are actors, actresses, columnists, producers, and an "optimistic" clergyman, "Looking, in his floppy matching slacks and shirt of jade-green silk, like a print I had once seen of the dowager of China, his wet underlip poised as if to receive a gumdrop, or to emit yet another platitude" (101-2). Carleton Burns, a completely obnoxious star, and an Italian sex queen, Gloria Mangiamele, are all brought together by Mason.

The exception to this group of pretenders is Cripps, the director, who, in conversation with Peter, gives a moral assessment of the crowd and particularly of the leading man, Carleton Burns: "A general wasting away of quality, a kind of sleazy common prostration of the human spirit. Like Burnsey there—a really sensitive decent guy beneath it all, and very close to a great actor. Yet what does he do? In his mid-thirties, just when an artist should be hitting his stride, achieving maturity, he sinks into this idiotic infantilism. He becomes a hipster. A juvenile delinquent. A dirty-mouth little boy" (116). These words of Cripps receive additional significance from the explosive appearance of Cass, who quotes Oedipus at Colonus while the ice cubes from his tilted glass perch "bizarrely on his eye-glasses." What has brought Cass to this point in his life and to the beginning of a way out of his prison of self-pity and flagellation becomes Styron's central concern in the remainder of the novel.

VII Cass Kinsolving's Guilt and Atonement

Through a number of confessional narratives, Cass reveals the sources of his guilt and paralysis. One confession in particular (368-78)—one in which he recounts the willful destruction of a Negro cabin—is directly connected with his one-man, foreign-aid program for the Valley of Tramonti (sunset). The valley seems "enchanted" at night, but the visible misery in the daytime makes it for Cass "the saddest place I know on earth." The home of the earth's miserable, it stands in direct contrast to Flagg's society of pointless hedonism. And, through Cass's·own guilt and remorse, he sees the valley as comparable to the lives of the Negroes whom he knew in the American South.

But these miserable Italian people, even in their misery—as Luigi, Cass's carabiniere friend, remarks—represent a "life force" with a far greater vitality than the Hollywood crowd. Their awareness of real pain and suffering is embodied in dying Michele, or in the ravished beauty, Francesca. Cass, to free himself by atoning for his crimes, at first performs for Flagg to get medicines for Michele; then, because he is tricked, he steals Flagg's medicines and food. After Peter and Cass visit the valley, Peter is awakened by the nightmare events of the rape, murder, and Flagg's apparent suicide. When Peter meets Cass, it is obvious that the artist has changed markedly: "Bloody with dazed and glassy eyes, he drew the children next to him in a smothering embrace. 'Press close to me on either side—' he began, then ceased. Abruptly, gently, he pushed them aside and struggled to his feet. He looked at me but he no longer saw me, I'm sure, his eyes fixed instead through me and beyond me upon some vista mysterious and distant and sufficient unto itself. His lips moved, but made no sound" (241). Even Cass's child-wife, Poppy, who generally shows a lack of comprehension, is impressed by this scene from *Oedipus*. Later, the full implications are clear: Cass has destroyed Mason Flagg.

Cass's confessions, which constitute Part Two of the novel, are heralded by Theodore Roethke's lines from "The Waking," [13] "I learn by going where I have to go." The quotation suggests that suffering and life experiences lead to awareness and that each man's way is his own. Experiences follow, visions of reality described by Cass with all the energy of his spirit; but there are side tracks. He looks at a street in Paris and makes it a part of himself: "It was no longer a street that I was watching; the street was inside my very flesh and bones, you see, and for a moment I was released from my own self, embracing all that was within the street and partaking of all that happened there in time gone by, and now, and time to come. And it filled me with the craziest kind of joy . . ." (257). This Whitmanian vision Cass wants to generate on canvas, but he cannot; the vision fades, but, for a moment, Cass has felt something like inspiration. The answer does not lie in romantic visions, however, but in self-discovery.

VII   Confessions, Dreams, and Nightmares

In contrast to the force of Cass's imagination, we have a story of failure with the girl evangelist. Told with the same crowding images of Peyton's confession, Mannix's stories of his brushes with death, and Nat Turner's recollections as he sits in his chains, Cass's expression is another clear demonstration of Styron's ability to create vivid character through poetic monologue. Cass's reminiscence of his sexual encounter with Vernelle Satterfield (259-67) and of her disappointment when "the divine spirit just flowed right on out" of him is linked in some inextricable way to his vision of the Paris street, for both experiences are examples of his inadequacy and his lack of control.

After his "vision" in Paris, Cass and his family of children move south through France; and he begins to keep a diary—

his first step toward self-analysis. Poppy is no help with her childlike faith, and Cass is intelligent enough to realize how inadequate her innocent belief would be for him. Eventually, they arrive in Rome and settle themselves in an apartment where Cass continues his work. But he has only reached a level above the abyss; his paintings are dull; he is still subject to fits of depression; the dark night of the soul is not half over.

Cass's encounter with the McCabes, a section of the novel which had appeared earlier,[14] is a significant regression for him. The McCabes represent the outer devil of Cass's hell, the nightmare horror of American society, just as Mason Flagg is part of Cass's inner horror later. Despite his loathing for the McCabes, Cass plays cards and drinks with them. Their mechanical, rapacious play infuriates Cass; and, angered by his waste of time, money, and spirit with the soulless McCabes, he explodes in rage. The card game and Cass's final explosive furor send him from the edge into the abyss; and he awakens twenty-four hours later, stripped, broken, and aching in a whorehouse outside Rome. Only his glasses are left him so that he can "see" himself as he is, helpless and exposed. Exhausted, he falls back into sleep and has his recurrent dream of the two landscapes. The romantic dream brings Cass to the edge of the abyss:

Here so familiar, was the black gulf, the solitary unpeopled coast rimmed round by palm trees, by the weathered slopes of volcanoes which from horizon to horizon sent plumes of smoke into a sickly overcast sky, devoid of sunlight, troubled by premonitions of thunder. Here on this gulf, in a tiny boat so frail that each black foamy wave threatened to swamp it, he was rowing with confused, exhausting strokes toward an island far out to sea where amid whirling carousels and orange blossoms and the black eyes of girls there existed a slumberous southern repose so sweet, so voluptuous, so soothing to his flayed and bedevilled senses that not to reach it would mean his ruin and his end. . . . In cataclysm, the great range of volcanoes erupted fire; the marvelous green coast or island, the enchanted land unseen at his back, perishing with its freight of unborn and untasted love, toppled into the sea with a hissing noise—"*Dio non esiste!*" he heard himself shriek—as at last one black and mountainous wave, washed to this gulf as if from the uttermost boundaries of the earth, bore him up and up through a sky snowy with the falling bodies of gulls, and descending now, onto the wretched and irremediable shore. . . . (310-11)

When Poppy comes to get Cass, his journey toward salvation has passed the last station before Sambuco. The whorehouse is located on the Via Appia, and the day is Good Friday.

On the day after Easter, overcome by a desire to escape, and seeking the "impossible prize or vision" of his dream, Cass journeys south on his motor scooter. His chance arrival in Sambuco takes on more significance in Cass's mind, for the town becomes the end of the line: "suddenly he was trapped, cornered, utterly hemmed in by Sambuco" (318). As if confirming this entrapment, Cass breaks a vase in the hotel. He becomes involved with the authorities, the girl Francesca, and the philosophical policeman, Luigi. His brief exchange with Luigi, the creative pessimist, convinces Cass to bring his family to Sambuco.

VIII   Remembrance of Crimes Past

Luigi replaces Cass's mentor Slotkin, the navy psychiatrist whose influence had developed Cass's enlightened view of himself; for Luigi gives Cass a more accurate view of the world around him and a way to cope with it. Luigi's philosophy of expediency is at first offensive to Cass's sense of "Anglo-Saxon self-righteousness," but his weakness and his desire to help the miserable poor of the Valley of Tramonti lead him to the very "expediency" that he despises. To free himself, Cass identifies the downtrodden of the Tramonti Valley with the Negroes. His attempt to save Michele by begging medicines from Flagg is one way of redeeming himself. With Mason's help, Cass gets medicines from an army PX. Surrounding him are all the manifestations of American opulence and insensitivity; and, forgetting his purpose, he breaks into drunken rebellion against these surroundings. In the end, he has to steal the drugs from Mason. These actions are the result of his compulsion to help the Italians, and its impetus lies in Cass's guilt-ridden memory of Crawfoot's cabin.

Describing the destruction of the Negro's cabin, Cass speaks of his sense of "righteousness" while he was caught in the momentum of his act. But the impression of guilt remains—and of the failure of any kind of amendment or atonement for such an act: "You live with it even when you've put it out of your mind —or think you have—and maybe there's some penance or justice in that" (379). Cass must work out his psychological struggle through action, and Albert Camus's remarks in *The Rebel* are significant here: "Every act of rebellion expresses a nostalgia for innocence and an appeal to the essence of being. But one day nostalgia takes up arms and assumes the responsibility of total guilt; in other words adopts murder and violence." [15] Camus's insight is directly relevant to Cass's assumption of "total guilt" and to the scenes of horror and violence which conclude Styron's novel.

IX Murder or Suicide?

In Chapter Ten, Cass recounts the gruesome ending to the events in Sambuco. He concludes that Mason's sexual needs demanded a violent rape and that Francesca was for Mason a substitute for Cass:

So that night, if you discount the business about the earrings and his rage over Francesca's alleged thievery—which was just a cover-up for something deeper—and put aside for a moment this theory about his impotence—which must be only part of the story—then you come up with one answer: he was raping ME. No, God knows I don't want to make it look like I'm transferring to myself any of that final and degrading suffering which Francesca endured alone. I just mean this, you see: he must have understood what was happening. He must have seen how things were shaping up. Because for more time than I care to think about I had allowed him to own me—out of spinelessness at first, out of whiskey-greed and desolation of the spirit, but at last out of necessity. And the paradox is that this slavish contact with Mason that I had to preserve in order to save Michele freed me to come into that knowledge of selflessness I had thirsted for like a dying man, and into a state where such a thing as dependence on the likes of Mason would be unheard-of, an impossibility. (443)

Cass recognizes Mason's fear that he was losing control over him: "by raping her [Francesca] he was raping the two of us: that night I felt he had committed some filthy, unspeakable violation upon life itself" (401). Cass then interprets the scene as that of the creative artist and the natural beauty (Francesca poses nude for him), both being violated by the symbol of a crass, evil, and impotent culture. Yet, even in his "foaming infuriate craze for revenge," Cass cannot conceive of murdering

Flagg until he hears of Francesca's murder. On the assumption that Flagg has killed her, Cass pursues the waiting child that Flagg has become, bashes in his skull, and casts him into the void.

It is clear that Cass is casting out the loathing devil of childishness which he sees in himself as well as in Mason: *" 'Children!'* he thought, standing erect over the twitching body. *'Children! My Christ! All of us!' "* (465). In speaking of the murder earlier, Cass says that murder is like an "amputation." By killing a man he "remove[s] part of . . . him[self] forever"; and Cass speaks more pointedly than he realizes: for Mason is the embodiment of the evil in Cass himself. When he describes Mason as a monster, Cass is unconsciously describing his own state. Only at the moment of the murder does Cass recognize the direct connection between himself and Mason, and only through the act itself can he exorcise his own devil. The confessional tone and the internal conflict have all the attributes of a psychodrama.

X Cass: The Absurd, Tragic, or Satiric Hero?

Throughout the novel Styron returns to the image of Oedipus as he did to a lesser degree in *Lie Down in Darkness* and in *The Long March.* In *Set This House on Fire,* Styron sees the figure of Oedipus in two extremes of character: Mason Flagg, the retarded Oedipus, remains forever a child who is hedonistic and pseudocreative; and Cass, the suffering Oedipus, is self-pitying, masochistic, and uncreative.[16] But to compare Cass to tragic figures or to regard *Set This House on Fire* as a tragedy can be misleading. Styron is using the trappings of tragedy, but his purpose is more satiric than tragic. The stage directions, for example, that Cass gives (*"Exeunt omnes.* Exit the whole lousy bunch" [239] sound like mock-tragedy. The one direct statement of tragic implication, besides Cass's absurd Oedipal performances, comes from Fausto Windgasser, the effeminate hotel proprietor, and it is hardly convincing: "Overpowring twagedy, my God. It's like the Gweeks, I tell you, but far worse!" (220). Windgasser, incidentally, refers to Cass as Mr. K. Though Cass's bombastic nature is hardly that of Kafka's hero, both share a burden of guilt and an acceptance of responsibility; but neither can be considered tragic figures.[17]

Cass's situation is not tragic; for, when all his defects are discovered and magnified, they are the flaws of his society. In this respect, Edwin Honig, in his study of allegory, *Dark Conceit*, makes a fundamental point about modern satire that illuminates Styron's technique:

the undercover means of effecting the distortion in satire are the same means by which something of the authority and values of heroic times —an otherwise forgotten Golden Age—is dramatically reinvoked. Such typical transformations are achieved in Swift and Kafka. But the ludicrous distortion of isolated defects we call caricature is not what Swift and Kafka aim at. For one thing, their distortions usually are far from being funny; for another, they exhibit not the isolated but the fundamental moral defects of all men living in society. How fundamental the defects are—or even that they exist—we seldom realize until we scrutinize them realistically, without vanity or other illusions. When we do examine them closely, the experience is so discomforting as to appear wholly monstrous—which is the very effect of Swift's and Kafka's distortions.[18]

In a perceptive analysis of *Set This House on Fire*, David Galloway regards the novel as an absurd tragedy in which Cass challenges the "purposive order of the universe, and in which right action is somehow rewarded and wrong action punished, if only within the confines of the individual conscience." At the end of the novel, Galloway says, "Cass must discover and shoulder his own sin, for there is no authority dictating punishment." [19] In other words, he must make fate a human concern. In support of arguments that Cass achieves a triumph over himself, Galloway makes frequent references to Camus's *Myth of Sisyphus*. This comparison is valid, especially since Styron has directly referred to Camus as an influence.[20]

Yet it is difficult to regard Cass's murder of Flagg as either a tragic or an absurd act since it is not a gratuitous or a fated action but a liberating one. Galloway sees the irony in the murder—"a conscious overt act in the name of order and value . . . [yet] a profound moral wrong . . . because he [Cass] has a sudden realization of Flagg's humaneness." [21] However, Flagg's murder is perhaps a symbolic act of suicide; it is the *only* means of Cass's freeing himself. The action is a necessary purge of the rebel, to move him from absurdity to rebellion. Although Galloway believes that, after the murder, Cass must choose between "suicide and life," he has made the choice already in murdering Flagg. In that action Cass sees that he has killed something in himself which had to be destroyed. His conversation later with Luigi is the rational counterpart to his action. Though Cass has relapsed into a sense of Puritan guilt, Luigi frees him with his rational argument.

XI Luigi as Cass's Virgil

The scenes with the rationalist Luigi are vital to an understanding of the novel; for, like Virgil with Dante, he guides Cass with the light of reason. But his advice is not important until after Cass's liberating act. Luigi's attacks on Northern European or American Puritanism are what we would expect, but they really have little effect on Cass until he commits the murder. Luigi's final speech to Cass is reminiscent of Hester Prynne's speech to Dimmesdale in Hawthorne's *The Scarlet Letter*.[22] Luigi speaks:

"Then consider this, too, my friend. Simply consider your guilt itself— your other guilt, the abominable guilt you have carried with you so long, this sinful guilt which has made you a drunkard, and caused you to wallow in your self-pity, and made you fail in your art. Consider this guilt which has poisoned you to your roots. Ask what it was. Ask yourself whether it is not better to go free now, if only so that you may be able to strike down this other guilt of yours and learn to enjoy whatever there is left in life to enjoy. Because if by now, through what you have endured, you have not learned something, then five years, ten years, fifty years in jail will teach you nothing." He came close to me. His face was shining with sweat. "For the love of God, Cass," he said. "Consider the *good* in yourself! Consider hope! Consider joy!" Then he stopped. "That is all I have to say. Now I am going to strike off that miracle." And he struck it off. . . . (499)

For Dimmesdale, it is too late; for Cass, it is not.

At the end, we are left with Cass's self-assessment. Freed by Luigi from being indicted for Mason's death, he is also released from being what Luigi terms "a damnable romantic from the north" with a "hideous sense of guilt." In their final conversation, Cass tells Peter that he has only reached a resting place:

Now I suppose I should tell you that through some part of suffering I had reached grace, and how at that moment I knew it, but this would not be true, because at that moment I didn't really know what I had reached or found. I wish I could tell you that I had found some belief, some rock, and that here on this rock anything might prevail— that here madness might become reason, and grief joy, and no yes. And even death itself death no longer, but a resurrection.

But to be truthful, you see, I can only tell you this: that as for being and nothingness, the one thing I did know was that to choose between them was simply to choose being, not for the sake of being, or even the love of being, much less the desire to be forever—but in the hope of being what I could be for a time. This would be an ecstasy. God knows, it would.

As for the rest, I had come back. And that for a while would do, that would suffice. (500-501)

And Cass continues in his last letter to remind Peter that he is only at the beginning ("A man doesn't even get started until he moves in toward *il mezzo del cammino*" [505]. In the epilogue, Cass has achieved the maturity (he quotes Edgar in *King Lear*: "ripeness is all" [506]), necessary to struggle with himself rather than indulge himself in self-pity; but the struggle continues as intensely as before. Styron places this kind of "being" against the nothingness, the suicidal childishness of Cass or, for that matter, of Flagg. At least that "paralyzing death of the soul . . . is pretty much gone" (8).

XII Psychodrama and Satire

We should not expect some profound philosophical truth in *Set This House on Fire*, for Styron is much more of a psychological than a philosophical novelist.[23] Neither is he a tragedian, despite the references to Oedipus. Indeed, Styron's whole approach to the situation is that of a satirist who employs the Gothic and grotesque to attack his subject, and the novel is as concerned with what is false in American life as it is with its central character. In fact, the two themes of social satire and personal tragicomedy are inextricably tied—and more successfully so, I believe, than in *Lie Down in Darkness* where family tragedy dominates the novel.

As Michel Butor writes in his incisive preface to the French edition: "We see that what is going on in the theatre of Sambuco is nothing less than an allegory of the American condition, an invitation to surmount it. It is not surprising that the author wrote in the first page of his book: 'The ambition of my enterprise has not prevented me from making many errors.' " [24] And there are errors in *Set This House on Fire*. Peter's father who helps deliver the condemnatory goods in the first pages disappears, having affected none of the action; the time shifts between Sambuco and South Carolina at times reduce the intensity of the macabre events of the murder; and Cass's self-pitying rhetoric often becomes vaporous. It is necessary to add, however, that that last stylistic difficulty is symptomatic of Cass's bedevilment before he begins to face reality. The rhetoric both characterizes his early condition and makes him a caricature, a satiric cartoon of Oedipus or of Lear. Yet, if we see the the novel in its fullest sense, with its elements of Gothic satire and of symbolic exorcism, it is much better than the judgment of its early critics made it appear.

One critic, Melvin J. Friedman, in the best early appraisal of Styron's work, was perceptive enough to see the possible link between Styron's technique and those of some contemporary French novelists. He suggests that the novel may be, in Sartre's expression, "a parody on the novel of 'quest,' " or a novel "devised almost in caricature of the straight unpretentious murder mystery." [25] Styron himself suggests elements of parody in the novel since Cass is proud of his role as a political cartoonist, considering himself "in a direct line of descent from Daumier and Rowlandson. . . ." "Who knows," Cass writes to Peter, "but whether it's the American Art form (not jesting . . .)" (8). Though Cass continues to paint in his spare time, he does find a great outlet in political and social satire.

In a sense, this assessment may be taken as Styron's view of the novel and also as an evaluation of his role as an "artist in bonds" in a false society. He has presented in a series of grotesque cartoons and characterizations the evils of mediocrity and of childish pretentiousness and, in the development of a hero, a satiric parable for the exorcism of these evils. Like William Faulkner, John Hawkes, and Nathanael West, Styron presents a comic-grotesque vision of the horror of the American Nightmare; and he offers symbolically the means to freedom— self-purgation.

In the figure of Cass Kinsolving and his rage, disgust, and despair with his society, we can see the links with Peyton, Mannix, and, more important, the evolution of the individual rebel. Although Cass is often an exaggerated caricature, he, in his rage and frustration, resembles Styron's latest and best rebel figure, Nat Turner.

CHAPTER 5

Rebellion and Redemption: The Confessions of Nat Turner

IN discussing Styron's newest novel, *The Confessions of Nat Turner*, it is essential to review his past work, those themes on which he has elaborated, his confessional technique, and his developing idea of the rebel hero. In both *The Long March* and *Set This House on Fire*, Styron energizes action, theme, and character beyond the doomed and static world of *Lie Down in Darkness*. The novels are also characteristic of Styron's struggle to free himself from the shadow of Faulkner and the classification of being a "Southern writer."

In all Styron's work there are strong moralistic convictions conveyed through the imagery of the Book of Revelations; through the mood of Greek tragedy; and, at times, through the introspective analysis of a seventeenth-century divine. Some critics may feel that Styron uses these elements almost as a set formula to appeal to a "middlebrow" audience.[1] But the fact remains that he is genuinely preoccupied with the chaotic state of American society, one in which social values and customs have been outworn and in which the highest value appears to be self-gratification. Styron offers no ideological panaceas in his work, except, by implication, an honest confrontation with our individual selves.

When Styron's fourth work of fiction, *The Confessions of Nat Turner*, appeared in the fall of 1967, the anticipated reaction from literary critics and social commentators was not so immediate as might have been expected. The general critical response was favorable, and the expected controversy did not materialize. However, after the initial reviewers had expressed their general approbation of the novel, a number of critics considered the social issue which the earlier reviewers had generally avoided. The social critics are not concerned with the technical or esthetic merits of Styron's novel so much as with what they consider to be his presentation of "white southern myths, racial stereotypes and derogatory literary clichés." [2] The article writers, like the reviewers before them, have completely ignored, however, Styron's themes and techniques in his earlier fiction as these relate to *The Confessions of Nat Turner.*

Whether an article is written from a sociological or a literary point of view, it is relevant that the critic examine the other works of a novelist before passing judgment on his current work. In fact, it is probably more significant in sociological criticism than in literary criticism since ideological comparisons often indicate how a writer arrived at such an opinion. The sociological critics of Styron's novel have preferred to begin with the fact of his being a white Southerner and to work from that viewpoint. But there is another approach to Styron's novel: an assessment of his past work in conjunction with *The Confessions of Nat Turner.* In Styron's preceding fiction, he developed particular themes on rebellion and the "System," his confessional technique, and the idea of a rebel-hero; and these relate to what he accomplishes in his 1967 novel.

I Styron's Earlier Novels

In Styron's earlier fiction he has two basic concerns: the condition of man in a fragmented society and the need for the individual to discover his own values and responsibilities. In his first three novels, the conflict is between man as he thinks he is and man as he discovers himself through honest experience. Though his characters are individualized in their situations, feelings, and actions, the major figures fall into three categories: a rebel-hero who is outraged at the falseness, purposelessness, and corruption of his society (Peyton Loftis, Mannix, Cass Kinsolving), but who is ignorant of his own weakness and involvement in that same society; an ineffectual, passive, but not unaffected observer (Milton Loftis, Culver, Peter Leverett), who is sympathetic to the rebel figure but who lacks his passionate rage; and, finally and the most abstract of all, a representative, monstrous at times, of the society and its evils who either hates or tries to control the rebel figure (Helen, Puritan-Romantic; Templeton, banality and military rigidity; Mason Flagg, self-gratification and sterility).

The society itself in Styron's earlier work is satirized; its superficial order only thinly covers the crowd of greedy, unhappy, and self-centered children underneath, as seen at Peyton's wedding or at Flagg's gathering. Yet the worst aspects are embodied in the almost monstrous cartoons Styron draws of the middle-class American mother, Helen Loftis, whose puritanical prurience destroys her and her family; the military mediocrity, Colonel Templeton, whose banality and mindless rule are ultimately destructive; and the grotesque, spoiled rich boy, Mason Flagg, whose affluence is used to buy or destroy the creativity of others. This criticism of American life, as seen through these characterizations; this satiric view of the general composition of the society; and Styron's eschatological imagery—all of these provide the background for the struggles of his individual rebel-heroes.

Styron's outraged heroes vary in their capacity to cope with this society, partially because they are ensnared by it. Peyton Loftis is conscious of the superficiality and condemns it in her mother's world as much as in the effete society of New York. Yet she cannot free herself from her own incestuous child's love for her father. Her promiscuity, which expresses her rebellion, leads to her suicide. Only her husband, Harry, is comparatively free; but he cannot be considered the novel's central consciousness. In *The Long March*, Mannix, like Harry, a Jew, consciously rebels against the system of the marines. Mannix's anger, though achieving more forceful proportions than Peyton's, becomes his solitary passion; and, in protesting the abstract evil of a non-human garrison state, he becomes a more fervid representative of its deadly banality than does its major exponent, Colonel Templeton.

With *Set This House on Fire*, as we have seen, Styron's Carolina mountain-man emerges more clearly as hero than do the major characters in the two earlier novels. Cass Kinsolving's anger is directed not only toward his society but toward himself, a new development in the Styronic hero from the rebellious figures of Peyton and Mannix. In destroying Mason Flagg, who, like Helen and Colonel Templeton, characterizes the evils of society, Cass frees himself from the possibility of the self-destructive and the futile action of Peyton and also from the partial failure of Mannix. Cass, at least, has learned by destroying the enemy within his limits and powers.

II The Expanded Character of the Rebel

The Confessions of Nat Turner displays a new range and scope in Styron's imagination. The next stage of his work was almost bound to involve the rebel-hero in an even more active struggle against the limitations placed on his soul by man himself and by the system. Styron has created his fullest character in Nat Turner, for his awareness and sensitivity to his situation surpass those of any previous Styron hero. In comparison to Peyton, who is pathetic, or to Mannix and Cass, who are often absurd or satiric, Nat assumes tragic proportions. Among the several reasons for this stature, not the least is the fact that Styron, through first-person narrative, identifies with Nat; for Nat's voice takes us through the novel, interpreting, reflecting, and re-enacting the rebellion.

In the issue of *Book Week* in which John Hope Franklin praised Styron's novel, Styron says in an interview that "The idea of telling Nat's story in the first person came to me suddenly five years ago. . . . I was reading Camus's *The Stranger*, here on Martha's Vineyard, and I made a connection. I said to myself, 'What a nice framework this would be. I can tell the story in the first person and have it end on the day of Nat's execution.' It was the final little peg I needed to begin writing." [3]

Alienated from blacks and whites, Nat is like Camus's Meursault in *L'Etranger;* but Nat's passivity turns to revolution. Meursault passively refuses to belong to a hypocritical society; Nat is excluded from it, but, more important, he is also excluded from love and thus he turns to revolution. In summary, Nat is the fully developed rebel figure who is no longer passive and whose ideology is personal action against a dehumanizing system. Indeed, Nat is a unique creation in American fiction.

Camus, referring to what he calls "the 'tough' [Hemingway] novel of the thirties and forties and not the admirable American efflorescence of the nineteenth century," attacked the so-called realistic American novel in a lengthy but very significant statement:

The American novel claims to find its unity in reducing man either to his elemental or to his external reactions and to his behavior. It does not choose feelings or passions . . . it rejects analysis and the search for a fundamental psychological motive. . . . This is why the unity of this novel form is only the unity of the flash of recognition. Its technique consists in describing men by their outside appearances . . . of reproducing, without comment, everything they say down to their repetitions. (Even in Faulkner, a great writer of this generation, the interior monologue only reproduces the outer husk of thought.) . . . It would seem that for these writers it is the inner life that tears people away from one another. This is a partially legitimate suspicion. *But rebellion, which is one of the sources of the art of fiction, can find satisfaction only in constructing unity on the basis of affirming this interior reality and not of denying it. To deny it totally is to refer oneself to an imaginary man.* [The italics are mine.][4]

Styron, in creating Nat Turner, affirms this "interior reality" through his personal identification with his character and through his creative imagination.

The double role of passive observer and rebellious hero, which are commingled in Nat, creates a tension in his character that is sustained throughout the novel. Styron's characters of outrage and passion in his previous novels exemplify his capability to confront and to overcome the psychological problem of portraying the mood of desperation, hatred, and violence of the Negro slave leader. Perhaps this capability can be demonstrated by comparing Nat's characterization with those of earlier novelists.

III   The Negro in Faulkner and in Earlier Novelists

In the work of Twain and Faulkner, as well as in that of Gertrude Stein, Sherwood Anderson, and Stephen Crane, there are examples of characterization of Negroes as individuals; but Camus's remarks deal primarily with the rebel figure in the novel—a role not generally associated with Negroes in American fiction until the 1930's. The passive role assigned to black men in fiction by the "Realists" was based partly on their general lack of knowledge about Negro life except on the most superficial level and partly on the general nostalgia for a simpler, less complex society. Faulkner and Anderson follow directly in Twain's path by generally regarding black men as enduring primitives. It is also true that Faulkner, in *Go Down Moses,* and Gertrude Stein in *Melanctha* both indicate an awareness and sensitivity about black men in a white-dominated society.

Styron, motivated by artistic as well as by personal and moral reasons, has created Nat Turner as an introspective hero who is in rebellion against his slavery—the "peculiar institution" of a false and corrupt society—yet who, despite the violence of his feelings, is capable of sympathy and even of love for his enemies. And Nat Turner is a markedly different character from those Negro figures of earlier American writers; for Harriet Beecher Stowe's Uncle Tom and Twain's Jim, who are mainly treated as individual characters, often appear also as stereotypes. In Mrs. Stowe's novel, Tom's function as a character is to exemplify the condition of "life among the lowly"; and, in *Huckleberry Finn*, Huck and Jim's relationship, shared experience, and mutual protectiveness bring out Huck's instinctive humanity. It is only natural that Jim is rarely "seen" internally since Huck is the central consciousness of the novel.

In *Light in August*, Faulkner never gets beyond Joe Christmas's crippling "doom" to present him as a fully developed character. For Joe is the sum and substance of what white Puritanism (North and South) has made him. Joe is never permitted, as Nat Turner is, to understand freedom; and he dies a sacrificial death for the sins of the community. We can sympathize with Joe, but it is difficult to empathize with him; instead, the reader is the observer who watches Joe's circular flight and the helplessness of those who want to help him.

IV The Negro in Postwar Fiction

Nat Turner is someone other than Jim or Joe Christmas, for Styron has permeated Nat's character with his own sense of outrage; and, in so doing, he involves the reader more directly. The confessional tone, which is not uncommon in contemporary fiction, is a technique that is natural to the novel of personal introspection and commitment. Parallels can be drawn with the work of several of Styron's contemporaries: Saul Bellow's *Adventures of Augie March*, Ralph Ellison's *Invisible Man*, Norman Mailer's *The Deer Park*, James Baldwin's *Giovanni's Room*.

Of the characters of these contemporary novelists, we might compare Nat Turner to the anonymous or unnamed character of Ellison's *Invisible Man* who also seeks his identity in revolutionary action. Ultimately aware that he and other individuals are being sacrificed to an ideological cause, Ellison's invisible hero leaves the Marxist movement. Like Nat, he acts out of a desire to discover his identity; and he ends with the realization that it has to be created. The other similarity between these two characters lies in their expectedly ironic attitude toward the white world and its hypocrisy. Such a comparison with Ellison's novel raises, however, the question of Styron's capability as a white man to understand and express this ironic attitude. Specific examination of Styron's novel and some of its sources should, hopefully, answer this question. Throughout the novel, Styron gives the sense of being so directly and personally involved in Nat Turner, that he regards him as an alter ego.

V "This Quiet Dust"

For Styron, writing *The Confessions of Nat Turner* was a moral and psychological need; and he so describes it in one of his best essays. In his essay, "This Quiet Dust" [5] and in a chapter of the novel published in the *Paris Review*, Styron declares his artistic desire and personal need to re-create Nat as a person. The connecting links with Nat's feelings, Styron declares, lie in his own guilt and responsibility as a white man in the South; and, to face his guilt and responsibility, he felt he had to identify as completely as possible with a slave of the early nineteenth century.

The novel is a fictional account of Nat Turner's slave rebellion in 1831, a subject which had interested Styron for several years;[6] and the fiction is based on accounts of the rebellion led by the educated slave preacher. Historically one of the few large Negro-organized slave rebellions, Nat's revolt probably came closer than any other to achieving success. The real Nat Turner, a skilled and inspired leader, was able to garner a sizeable force of fifty slaves and to capture a number of plantations before being stopped by the militia. His rebellion brought about severe repercussions; and, though Turner thought of his revolt as local, it led to severe laws in Southern states regarding slaves. Most historians feel that the rebellion caused masters to use even more repressive measures to keep their slaves in line. This repression resulted in a greater reaction against the inhumanity of slavery and thereby hastened the Civil War.[7]

There is a curious ambiguity in Styron's essay about his return to the Virginia Tidewater country which he made in connection with his work on the novel. Despite the tranquil title of his essay, "This Quiet Dust," Styron's key point is change; and the undercurrent of violence is in the air. Styron recounts the historical Nat Turner rebellion, the present-day white Southerners' (including his own) reactions to it, and its effect on the Negro's role, then and now, in Southern life. Yet Styron is more concerned with the ambivalent attitude of "enlightened" Southerners who deplore the mistreatment of black men but still argue that the Negroes are inferior. This ambivalence, he tells us, is the result of the white Southerner's inability to "know" Negroes.

As an example, Styron compares his experience with that of Faulkner, who "confessed a hesitancy about attempting to 'think Negro' and whose Negro characters . . . seem . . . meticulously *observed* rather than *lived*" (italics Styron's). Styron distinctly wished to "recreate and bring alive that dim and prodigious black man" [8] and to attempt what Faulkner did not try. For instance, in the novel Styron presents Nat as a heroic individual, not as the abstract primitive consciousness of Faulkner's slave in "Red Leaves." Indeed, Nat is a sophisticated, articulate Western man who, having benefited from education and knowledge, is conscious of the freedom that was his human right as a man, black or white. This approach requires a different sense of the Negro from that of Faulkner, whose view was that Negroes were "gradually" to be allowed equal status. Styron believes that the "moral imperative" of every white Southerner is to "know" Negroes, even if the desire may be resented as "outrageous condescension" and even if it is probably too late. And "knowing" involves an empathetic identification with a character.

Styron considers his work "a very modern novel." When he states that man must "give up his individual liberty to live in the way he wants to live," Styron echoes one of his main themes: the realization of self and the awareness of limitation. In Nat's life, rebellion means that he can no longer desire freedom for himself alone and that nothing less than the end of a dehumanizing system will suffice. Yet it is important to remember that his shift from passive anticipation of freedom to revolutionary struggle is motivated by the inhuman social strictures against personal love and manhood that have been placed upon him by the slave system.

VI Theological and Historical Implications

Styron also recognized the theological implications of his novel, for Turner is seen as a Christian—at times, he is like Milton's hero in *Samson Agonistes*—who is forcibly contending with the evils of his society. Since Nat regards himself as a Christian hero who is freeing the black slaves under God's direction, the religious nature of Nat's character cannot be over-emphasized. Styron, in explaining the design of the novel and his use of retrospection, speaks of this religious element: "The major reason, however, was that I wanted to get Nat after the insurrection, when he was questioning the entire relationship he had with God, with the God who had been his guide and mentor and light throughout his life as a preacher. I wanted to discover what was going on in his mind, now that he had insti-gated and committed murder, and now that he is bereft of God. The relationship with God seemed to be the central thing in my own conception of the man." [9]

As for the historical implications, Styron commented, in an-swer to a question about his remark that America has lived outside the main current of history, that "We have never recog-nized until recently that the obvious stream of history could be in great measure the story of what happens when X million Africans rise up and assert themselves." [10] Clearly, Styron re-gards Nat Turner's story as a microcosm of what is occurring in contemporary history.

In a review written earlier about Herbert Aptheker's *American Negro Slave Revolts,* Styron approached the question of Negro stereotypes that range from Stowe's Uncle Tom to Mailer's "White Negro." Because he felt that Aptheker, in his efforts to counter the false racial arguments of older historians such as U. B. Phillips, had overstated the case for Negro revolts, Styron suggested that Stanley Elkins's "brilliant analysis" in *Slavery* gave a far more accurate picture of what the slave system did to human beings. Styron states in his review that rather than create the spirit of revolution, the system had a traumatizing effect which dehumanized the slave. Further, Styron continues, the fact that plantation slaves were docile was not so much a commentary on the Negroes' character as a tribute to a "capitalist super-machine which swiftly managed to cow and humble an entire people with a ruthless efficiency. . . ."

Styron's descriptions of this system and its effects on individual slaves in *The Confessions of Nat Turner* have a power of reality and conviction in them as telling as any historical account. In his characterization of Nat, Styron shows the effect of the system on a human being; and his persuasiveness comes from his identification with his slave hero. While Styron relies on personal identification and moral imagination to create his central character, he has drawn on historical sources for his account of the slave system. In his review of Aptheker's book about Negro slave rebellions, Styron agrees with Aptheker that slave rebellions had not, except for Turner's and Vesey's, been of significant size. He differs with Aptheker's position that the slaves were only held back from rebellion by a lack of physical power and organization; for in substantial agreement with Stanley Elkins (whose book on slavery he praises), Styron believes that the system brutalized men spiritually and he draws an analogy, as does Elkins, to the victims of Nazi camps who did not revolt.[11]

Elkins develops the camp-prisoner and slave parallel much further in his book *Slavery: A Problem in American Institutional and Intellectual Life.* Although he is careful to make several important distinctions between the camp prisoners and the slaves (secret nature of the camps, no private life for prisoners, and prisoners' state of chronic hunger), Elkins does demonstrate a great number of similarities. The most significant of these were the childlike qualities adopted by the inmates, the identification with their captors, and their attitude toward their guards or masters as father symbols. The prisoners' experiences matched those of the slaves: there were few cases of real resistance, considering the slaves' number and comparative freedom; few suicides; and an absence of general hatred for the S.S. (*Schutzstaffel*) and the master. Both the concentration camp and the slave system were "closed systems" from which all standards based on prior connections had been effectively detached. A working adjustment to either system required a childlike conformity, a limited choice of what Elkins calls "significant others" (besides one's immediate family). Resistance within such a closed system was, Elkins concludes, highly improbable, since the victims in both instances were brainwashed and dehumanized.

The basis for both systems was a rigid ideology which considered the victims as inferior racially (through Nazi race theories and Calvinistic religious attitudes toward blacks) and as nonhuman beasts. In contrast, large-scale and heroic black revolutions took place in Latin America where slaves were allowed participation in the society; they had legitimate roles and functions outside of the plantation. Freedoms like these which allowed for personality development were rarely given American slaves and the Nat Turners were the exception that proved the rule.[12] And it is with Nat Turner's psychological growth that Styron is primarily preoccupied; secondarily, Styron is concerned with the system Nat opposed.

VII "The Real Revolt"

The real revolt lies in Nat's assertions of *self*. He is an individual who represents the aspirations of all men held in slavery who conceive of freedom:

Nat Turner, a literate preacher and a slave of the Upper South, lived outside the thralldom of organized plantation slavery; the success of his revolt was due to a combination of native genius, luck, and the relative latitude of freedom he had been granted. The many millions of other slaves, reduced to the status of children, illiterate, tranquilized, totally defenseless, ciphers and ants, could only accept their existence or be damned, and be damned anyway, like the victim of a concentration camp. Rebellion was not only not characteristic: to assign a spirit of rebelliousness to human beings under such conditions is to attribute to the Negro super-human qualities which no human being possesses. Like the comic chicken thief, like the raging hipster, the slave in revolt is a product of the white man's ever-accommodating fantasy, and only the dim suggestion of the truth. The real revolt, of course, is now, beyond the dark wood of slavery, by people reclaiming their birthright and their direct, unassailable humanity.[13]

It is this humanity that Nat's character specifically personifies, with all the conflicting elements of savage hatred, charity, violence, and love. For Nat is a complicated character, not a stereotype, even in the original *Confessions*.[14] For Styron to re-create Nat, he had to identify with him; and, for a writer whose hero is invariably a rebel against a closed system, Nat is a natural subject.

In "This Quiet Dust" Styron begins, as we have noted, with a discussion of his commitment to a "moral imperative" to "know" Nat Turner as a man. The rest of the essay deals with the mood and the feeling that surround that search and the effect of memory and incident on Styron's mind: his return to Southampton was "not for the facts" but for the atmosphere of the adjacent countryside and the mood of the people who live there. In his description is that same graphic and immediate mood that Styron creates in his other work.

After quoting from Nat's description in the original *Confessions*, of the murder at the Travis house, the place of Nat's only killing, Styron reiterates the mood of conscience, guilt, and responsibility which provides the connection between his consciousness and that of Nat Turner: "It is Nat's only murder. Why from that point on does the momentum of the uprising diminish, the drive and tension sag? Why, from this moment in the (original) *Confessions*, does one sense in Nat something dispirited, listless, as if all life and juice had been drained from him . . . ? What happened to Nat in this place? Did he discover his humanity here, or did he lose it?"[15] Around this question Styron draws the character of his rebel-hero and provides the moral center for his novel.

At the end of his essay, Styron quotes a poem of Emily Dickinson, similar to the one he recalls in *The Long March*, that reflects both the repose of death and the current of life, violence, and change: "This quiet Dust was Gentlemen and Ladies, / And Lads and Girls; / Was laughter and ability and sighing, / And frocks and curls." The resulting poetic tension corresponds to Styron's feelings as he viewed the still countryside in which bloody events had occurred.

VIII   "Judgment Day"

The Confessions of Nat Turner marks a distinct but natural development in Styron's work, and his hero emerges in his individual rage and in the personal assertion of his humanity. The title is indicative of the new hero, who, though tortured by self-doubt, remains true to his own feelings and responses. He is never contrite. In the novel Styron manages to maintain the unremorseful and straightforward tone of Nat's own expression just as it is in the original *Confessions*. Depending on the situation, the fictional Nat Turner uses the language and tone of Bunyan's *The Life and Death of Mr. Badman,* the Bible, or the slave vernacular. Nat Turner is most convincing when he speaks in the tones of the first two styles, for Styron is intelligent enough not to relate too much of his novel through the vernacular of nineteenth-century slave dialect.

The opening note of the novel is struck by the voice of T. R. Gray, Nat's confessor. Gray visits him in prison for the sole purpose of taking Nat's confessions which, he hopes, will remove "doubts and conjectures" about the rebellion, show the true dangers, and reduce the fears of the white community. Gray regards himself as the reasonable eighteenth-century man dealing with what he considers the evil of "gloomy fanaticism." For Gray, the *Confessions* has a social value of solving the mystery of the rebellion by declaring it an "awful lesson" of a mind tending to grapple with problems beyond its capability and of one that is "the offspring of gloomy fanaticism." Since the *Confessions* was to show the rebellion as an aberration and to calm the fears of the whites, Gray uses every kind of cajolery and threat to compel Nat to confess. Gray is the spokesman for a society which must retain control at any cost, which must quell passion and fear in whites as well as in blacks, and which views men not as individuals but as members of a closed, rigid society.

In sharp distinction, Nat's character from the very beginning is one of passion and imagination. The first part of his narrative, "Judgment Day," is a dream in which Nat is drifting in a boat past a cliff, "the last outpost of land." The atmosphere is "seasonless," neutral; the boat drifts toward "the infinite vastness of blue water stretching out to the limit of the eye." Atop the promontory is a temple, without windows or columns or doors, "a temple in which no one worships": "or a sarcophagus in which no one lies buried, or a monument to something mysterious, ineffable, and without name. But as is my custom whenever I have this dream or vision, I don't dwell upon the meaning of

the strange building standing so lonely and remote upon its
ocean promontory, for it seems by its very purposelessness to be
endowed with a profound mystery which to explore would yield
only a profusion of darker and perhaps more troubling mysteries,
as in a maze" (4).

This temple seems to enclose the mystery of origin, the un-
knowable mystery of existence, the womb of timelessness. Nat's
dream is almost synonymous with that described in a different
context in Freud's *The Interpretation of Dreams:* "In dreams as
in mythology, the delivery of the child *from* the uterine waters
is commonly presented by distortion as the entry of the child
into water; [from] river to ocean in this case, the ocean being
freedom to expand his [soul] the births of Adonis, Osiris, Moses,
and Bacchus are well known illustrations of this." [16]

The sea which entices Nat is the symbol of the expanding
spirit which he feels. But this spirit, like the sea, he has yet to
view. Styron's juxtaposition of dream and reality, with which
he effectively began *The Long March,* is employed advanta-
geously here; for Nat awakens from his dream so weighted with
chains that he is unable to put his feet on the floor. The sounds
of his lieutenant, Hark, in the next cell and of a distant horn
calling slaves to early morning labor also form a sharp contrast
to Nat's poetic dream vision. The implications of the dream,
which recurs throughout the novel, are significant in Nat's desire
for freedom and of his movement toward a liberation of his
spirit to the open sea "faintly booming and imminent yet without menace." The temple, both womb and grave, is mysterious
in its "purposelessness."

Nat, who is imprisoned in the Jerusalem jail, is isolated from
men and not allowed his Bible; and he senses the totality of
his separation from men and God. Like Milton's *Samson,*[17] Nat
feels the bitterness of being delivered into the hands of his enemies partly through the failure of his own people to help him.
Despite his despair, he begins his trials with a small but important victory. Gray, who desires Nat's confession, has waited
five days for Nat to agree. When Nat finally does agree, he
does so partially because of his and Hark's physical pain and
mainly because he can yet derive some value from a confession.
Nat describes a "vision" in which God tells him "Confess, that

all nations may know. Confess, that thy acts may be known to all men." In his joy in getting Nat's confession, Gray misses the irony in Nat's statement: "not confess your sins, sir. . . . There was no *confess* your sins at all. *Confess, that all nations may know* . . ." (15). But Nat's assertion of himself is partly offset by Gray's mocking reminder of his failure: "It was them other niggers that cooked your goose, Reverend" (23).

Alone, "motionless in my web of chain," Nat compares his lot to a fly caught in the hell of "a blind and automatic obedience to instinct." Although Nat rejects this view as invalid for him (he thinks of suicide as an act of *his* will), it brings out the bitter- ness he feels toward "my black shit-eating people [who] were surely like flies, God's mindless outcasts, lacking even that will to destroy by their own hand their unending anguish . . ." (27). The Negroes' Christian faith, the stoic acceptance of suffering, and their patience and forbearance were not what kept them from action; it was their own sloth and fear. Nat's despair, which "lay deeper than madness," has its roots in the failure of his rebellion to create the desire for freedom in others—for a free- dom based on a man's sense of himself as a human adult, not as a childlike chattel. The world about Nat regards him as a chattel; even the indictment of the rebels is governed by economic con- siderations, since many of the younger, healthier slaves are re- turned to their masters so that there is no additional "property" loss. But the rebellion has shattered faith in the slaves' com- placency, and Gray's anxiety to re-create the image of the black men as irrational animals shows how a planned, intelligent rebellion for human freedom by black men threatens the entire system.

In this opening section entitled "Judgment Day," Nat and his confessor, T. R. Gray, face each other: the rebel is struggling to be more than a "mindless outcast," to free himself and his fellow slaves, to fulfill the mission which God had given him and his adversary; and the community prosecutor, Gray, arguing nineteenth-century "scientific" racial theories, cites Leibnitz as a defense of order and the status quo. Later, when one of the magistrates, Trezevant, compares Nat to Attila and to Genghis Khan, he is only echoing the apprehensions of Gray and of the community who regard Nat as a fanatic, a dangerous "enthusiast." This confrontation with the community has its ironies, and they reveal the wide differences between Nat and Gray. Neither of them is ignorant or unintelligent; they are just widely disparate in their views of reality. Though Gray may lack feeling at times, he is not a stereotyped villain. Like Colonel Templeton in *The Long March*, he has his version of truth; and he remains rigid in his convictions.

IX   Nat as God's Child

Nat changes, however, not in his version of the truth but of himself. During the novel, Styron enlarges his portrayal of Nat through his reflections and introspections as Nat develops, again like Samson in Milton's poetic drama, a new awareness of his relation to God. To understand Nat's personal and religious redemption, we must recognize that his God is the Judaic-Christian combination of the avenging arbiter who frees his people from their bondage and of the figure of love, charity, and human fellowship. The tension between these two views of God and Nat's resolution of this tension are the main substance of Styron's novel. Historically, Nat appears motivated primarily by a messianic or prophetic power which he attributes to God's election of him. Styron, intrigued by Nat's murder of Margaret Whitehead, recognizes that Nat is not merely a "gloomy fanatic"; he is also a human being who can be moved by the power and force of love.

When Styron describes Nat's feelings in prison, he draws on an actual situation involving Ben Reid, a black man condemned to death by the people of Connecticut. In a straightforward, unsentimentalized account, Styron described the case in two *Esquire* magazine articles [18] which are partially directed against the evils of capital punishment. Of greater importance is Styron's condemnation of a society which sentenced Reid to a life of poverty, neglect, and futility by giving him a set of social values which excluded him from that social system. Particularly, however, Styron writes in terms of Nat's mood of the condemned man: "It may be said perhaps that in prison a man's identity cannot be much, but we who are on the outside looking in—we who are so prone to forget that all men must be given at least the possibility of redemption—are in no position to judge." [19] While in prison, Nat achieves his full sense of identity, like

Camus's Meursault in *The Stranger,* and thus achieves his redemption. Like Ben Reid, Nat grows in prison, though Nat began developing earlier while in slavery, to emerge as a larger person than his captors who are still caught in the slavery of their unimaginative sterile lives.

X   Jeremiah Cobb and Margaret Whitehead

The confessions which Nat dictates to Gray begin with his origins. Through a simple flashback (simple compared to the use of flashback in *Lie Down in Darkness* or *Set This House on Fire*), Styron has Nat emotionally enlarge on the sparse details he relates to Gray. As Nat dictates, he is aware of Hark's cries in the next cell, of Negro children laughing and playing as they come out of a wood, of whites passing along the village street on the way to the trial, and, finally, of the memory of his first meeting with his trial judge, Jeremiah Cobb.

The windy, desolate November day on which Nat remembers meeting Jeremiah Cobb is a particularly sharp recollection. While he is considering on that day the words of the Prophet Ezekiel, "Slay utterly old and young, both maids and little children, and women; but come not near any man upon whom is the mark . . ." (of those who "cry for all the abominations" [52]), Nat looks from a knoll at the countryside he intends to invade and pillage. His bloody thoughts are further enraged by Hark's obsequiousness before Cobb, who encounters the two slaves while they are skinning rabbits. Nat sees the fear in Hark's face:

He had the face one might imagine to be the face of an African chieftain—soldierly, fearless, scary and resplendent in its bold symmetry—yet there was something wrong with the eyes, and the eyes, or at least the expression they often took on, as now, reduced the face to a kind of harmless, dull malleable docility. They were the eyes of a child, trustful and dependent, soft doe's eyes mossed over with a kind of furtive, fearful glaze, and as I looked at them now—the womanish eyes in the massive, sovereign face mooning dumbly at the rabbit's blood—I was seized by rage. (56)

Nat's rage is twofold—anger at the whites for making Hark into something less than a man and at Hark for his acceptance of their intent. This rage alienates Nat from his fellow slaves, and his is a justifiable rage against a society in which he can never be a human being in the full sense of the word. The rage has its source in Nat's individual feelings as a man, not in any ideology or religious belief. His religious and intellectual energies may channel and direct this rage, but its source lies in Nat's particular psychological development.

Affected by Cobb's surprising declamation against the evil slave system which also tortures him, Nat promises himself to follow Ezekiel's words and spare "any man upon whom is the mark." Yet the day of the trial finds Nat and Cobb facing each other across the bar of justice; and both men are condemned to die shortly: Nat, by hanging; Cobb from disease. Cobb has remained the observer in the trial; and though, as in his original statement at the real trial,[20] he expresses sympathy for Nat, the enormity of the crime is such that he condemns Nat to death.

The trial itself provides an ironic counterpoint to Nat's thoughts. While Trezevant reads Nat's confessions in order to play on the crowd's emotions, Nat reflects on the isolation of Job, on his "abandonment" by God, and on his own need for a Bible; and, while Gray draws on racial theories and eighteenth-century mechanistic philosophy to assuage the white community's fears of black insurrection, Nat remembers Margaret Whitehead, his one victim and the object of his love-hate for whites.

Margaret, a curious combination of sensitivity and Christian sentimentality, touches Nat with the possibilities of freedom more than any other character in the novel. In this early scene, Styron presents her as a chattering, naïve girl who is insensitive to Nat's feelings about her:

I am filled with a bitter, reasonless hatred for this innocent and sweet and quivering young girl, and the long hot desire to reach out with one arm and snap that white, slender, throbbing young neck is almost uncontrollable. Yet—strange, I am aware of it—it is *not* hatred; it is something else. But what? What? I cannot place the emotion. It is closer to jealousy but it is not even that. And why I should feel such an angry turmoil over this gentle creature baffles me, for save for my one-time master Samuel Turner, and perhaps Jeremiah Cobb, she is the only white person with whom I have experienced even one moment of a warm and mysterious and mutual confluence of sympathy. Then all at once I realize that from just that sympathy, irrestible on my

part, and unwanted—a disturbance to the great plans which this
spring are gathering together into a fatal shape and architecture—
arises my sudden rage and confusion. (92)

It is that sympathy and pity that he most detests and needs
from Margaret. And it is that rage which he and his co-conspir-
ators feel when Nat remembers their making their plans. A few
seconds before the court passes sentence Nat banishes Will and
the others from his mind as he recalls Margaret at the "mission"
service for the blacks. His hatred for the dull, stolid faces of
his fellow slaves is changed to love by the sight of Margaret.
Her sensitivity to the "folderol" of the white man's sermon meant
to keep the slaves apathetic and submissive and her inability to
be able to express her feelings mark her as someone partly
estranged from white society. Yet in her naïveté she is the most
enraging white of all; for she can attract and affect Nat, seem to
promise freedom and love, and then destroy that promise through
her own inadequacy.

The section closes with Gray's reappearance in Nat's cell after
the trial. Just as he tempts Nat before the trial with the failure
not only of his mission but of each of the slaves who joined him,
so does Gray taunt Nat now with the failure of God and Christianity. Though it is doubtful that Gray discusses with Nat the
effect of astronomy on the belief in God in the eighteenth and
nineteenth centuries, what he does express is the rationalistic
and practical view that Christianity and "divine guidance" were
no longer valid. By the end of his argument, Gray is successful
in shattering Nat's faith that what he is doing is "Holy Will" and
that his rebellion has been what Gray calls "a pissy-assed record
of total futility." Like Samson and Job, Nat does not lose faith
in God but seeks redemption, though he has no idea from where
it will come. In Milton's drama, Samson is redeemed because,
in his final action, he does act as God's agent; and Job *does
succeed* by hearing directly from God. But redemption for Nat
must be found in his past actions, and he is forced to reflect on
the meaning and relevance of all his experience.

XI "Old Times Past"

The second section of the novel, "Old Times Past," is recounted
in straight first-person narrative by Nat. In this section, Styron

reviews the basic tensions of Nat's past which brought him to rebellion. To put it simply, they are the tensions which result when a human being is placed in a hopeless situation, given the smallest morsel of hope, and then has it denied him. Beginning with his visits to the grave of his grandmother, who went mad in captivity after giving birth to Nat's mother, his disgust and horror at watching the primal scene of his mother and the brutish white overseer, and his memory of his father's flight from slavery, Nat realizes early in life the impotence, monotony, and misery of slave life. His only compensation is that he is a household slave and that, as yet, he is not expected to work.

The morsel of hope begins with Nat's desire to learn to read, an ambition encouraged by his master, Samuel Turner. His brother Ben regards Sam's efforts to educate and train slaves for emancipation as sentimental and unrealistic. Yet both brothers consider Nat as a "thing"; and, though Nat does not realize it at the time, there is no question about what will happen when an economic depression forces Samuel Turner to sell him,

Nat, unfortunately but quite naturally, regards Samuel Turner as a father figure; and, to complicate matters, he falls in love with Miss Emmeline, whom he worships "with a chaste, evangelical passion." During his adolescence, Nat Turner discovers the shortcomings of his white "parents"; and the tensions which inexorably create the frustrations of his life become more evident. For, much as he is drawn to Samuel Turner, he becomes more and more aware of what his position as a slave really means. By the age of sixteen, he is disabused of his illusions about Emmeline when he overhears her sexual encounter with her cousin, a scene sharply reminiscent of the one between his mother and the overseer. Worse, he is again reminded of his position: "This is what comes of being a nigger. It ain't fair. If I wasn't a nigger I wouldn't find out about things I don't want to find out about. It ain't fair" (181). What Nat Turner unconsciously objects to is the end of innocence, a discovery that there is a correlation with Nat's other discoveries about human relationships: knowledge and experience bring suffering.

XII The Promise of Freedom

Styron continually underscores Nat Turner's separation from the other slaves. Assigned to repair their cabins, he finds them repulsive and simultaneously feels shame at being a Negro. Yet all these conflicts in Nat are momentarily dispelled by Samuel Turner's promise of freedom to Nat as they journey into town. The woods provide an ironic setting: passing deer, seeking forage, remind Nat's master not of free, natural creatures but of the hard times that have come to the land and of the fact that such economic conditions will mean the sale of slaves southward. But Nat hears little of this news; and minutes later, still exhilarated by Turner's promise of freedom, Nat is unaffected by the appearance of a slave coffle headed further south. The bitter words of one of the slaves, however, revive the ominous threat to Nat's hope of freedom. What is implied is what Nat must learn: there is no freedom for a man as long as the system enchains other men.

The promise of Nat's freedom fills him with religious fervor and naturally affects his attitude toward his fellow slaves. His love for Willis and their dedication to Christian endeavor are the result of Nat's new outlook. But again events presage Nat's own situation when Willis is sold by the Turners. Despite his bitterness about Willis's sale, Nat remains optimistic about his own future. Even when the Turner slaves and estate are sold for debts, he is still promised freedom by his master. Yet, in the end, Turner cannot keep his word, and Nat remains a slave. His new master, the Reverend Eppes, a homosexual, tries to "ravish" Nat; but he ends by only exploiting him by hiring him to others. Ultimately sold by Eppes, Nat appears in the last scene of the section as he lies in a wagon, driven by two illiterate white traders, on his way to Southampton County.

XIII "Study War"

Part Three ("Study War") of the *Confessions* begins with a description of the hatred which Negroes have for whites; this hatred, which is based on knowledge, is therefore more genuine than that based on the fear of the unknown:

For without knowing the white man at close hand, without having submitted to his wanton and arrogant kindnesses, without having smelled the smell of his bedsheets and his dirty underdrawers and the inside of his privy, and felt the casual yet insolent touch of his women's fingers upon his own black arm, without seeing him at sport and at ease and at his hypocrite's worship and at his drunken vileness and at his lustful and adulterous couplings in the hayfield—without having known all these cozy and familial truths, I say, a Negro can only *pretend* hatred. Such hatred is an abstraction and a delusion. (257-58)

The result of Nat's frustrations is a single-minded hatred, and he begins to plan the destruction of the whites. He seeks out those Negroes who hate, as he does, because of their intimate, direct knowledge of whites.

Styron's psychological attitude is based on a belief that hate and love are not abstractions but are based on concrete reality and experience. When Nat describes "knowledge" as the basis for hate, we are reminded that Styron also sees it as the basis for love. It is through the examination of the peculiar nature of the love-hate relationship that Nat Turner comes to a realization, by the novel's end, of his redemption.

Easily one of the most powerful incidents in Nat's probe is a scene which occurs fairly early in Part Three. A beautiful Northern lady arriving to marry one of the wealthy landowners asks directions of an ancient freedman, Arnold. To Nat Turner and the other slaves, Arnold is a symbol: he represents the incarnation of freedom, a "freedom" of the illiterate, unskilled man left to beg and grovel and to depend on the pity of white men. Arnold's "freedom" is worse than slavery.

Arnold is incapable of speaking or understanding clearly what the woman asks him. She becomes confused and upset by his inarticulate mumble; and, in a fit of horror, guilt, and remorse, she strikes herself in an "angry, tormented gesture." The whole scene awakens a "hot convulsive emotion" in Nat:

For what I had seen on this white woman's face was pity—pity wrenched from the very depths of her soul—and the sight of that pity, the vision of that tender self so reduced by compassion to this helpless state of sobs and bloodless clenched knuckles and scalding tears, caused me an irresistible, flooding moment of desire. And it was, you see, pity alone that did this, not the woman herself apart from pity. . . . It was as if, divesting herself of all composure and breaking down in this fashion—exposing a naked feeling in a way I had never seen a white woman do before—she had invited me to glimpse herself naked in the flesh, and I felt myself burning for her. Burning! (263-64)

Louis Rubin, in an excellent review[21] of Styron's book, cites this episode as one of the best in the novel because it portrays

Nat's madness over the "occasional expression of pity" of white people. To this observation I would add that Nat's hatred and feelings of physical violence reflect not only his past experience with his insincere "master-father" but also his desire to break through the wall of sentimentality and guilty fear and to force his physical self on whites. Indeed, Nat's situation parallels that of Mannix in *The Long March* when he becomes the faceless marine machine in his mania to destroy his enemy, Colonel Templeton. Similarly, Nat desires to force his body on the distraught Northern lady. Both rebel heroes lose themselves in passionate rage against an abstracted "enemy," and, though Mannix's and Nat's rages are directed at two different "systems," they both momentarily lose their identities in their anger. "And it was *pity* alone that did this, not the woman herself apart from pity," says Nat (italics mine, 264). Nat Turner's rage becomes an obsessive irrational force that attacks "pity," not the woman.

This incident more than any other gives the motive for Nat's actions, and it also demonstrates a more complicated development in Styron's rebel-hero. Peyton, Mannix, and Cass may identify with their enemies—Helen, Templeton, and Mason Flagg; and they may eventually hate themselves for it. In the case of Cass and Mannix, however, they arrive at a point where self-discovery leads to redemption. But Nat is too bound up with his "enemy," the Northern white women, Miss Emmeline, and finally with Margaret Whitehead, the victim of his one and only murder. This complicated relationship Styron epitomizes in this one striking scene with the Northern woman which is connected directly to the sacrifice of Margaret at the close of the novel.

Nat is troubled by his response to the scene: "It was not a white person's abuse or scorn or even indifference which could ignite in me this murderous hatred but his pity, maybe even his tenderest moment of charity" (267). Nat's response is honest, for the surest means of arousing hatred is the demeaning condescension of sentimentalized pity. The paradox of the situation is that such pity serves to remind Nat of his condition; it takes him to the edge of love but goes no further.

Fulfilling his role as the humble slave, Nat serves his time with his new owner, Moore. In isolated moments, he reads the

Prophets of the Old Testament (when he was with Samuel Turner, he had read the Psalms; now he reads Ezra and Isaiah). Separated by his hatred from the whites, Nat becomes closer to his fellow slaves, particularly to Hark. He begins to preach to the slaves on the need for pride in themselves as men.

But Nat's real drive begins when famine strikes the land, and he gradually begins to see the whites as less powerful than he had thought. When Isham, a free Negro, who is driven by madness and hunger, curses Nat's master, Nat discovers that Moore lives in deadly fear of the Negroes' anger and that the passionate rage of a starving man can terrorize one of the masters and send him dashing away in fear. As a result of Isham's proud defiance and stand as a man, Nat intensifies his hatred of the white man's bondage. After Nathaniel Francis, the cruelest of the slave owners, has forced his slaves to fight one another for his amusement, Nat preaches to the slaves and holds them momentarily with his rage. Some turn away, but many remain; and Nat discovers his power to convince men.

His preaching affects a white man, a sodomite named Brantley, who can get no help from the white minister. Despite his disgust with Brantley and the risk to his own situation, Nat baptizes him in a pond while the white spectators throw stones from the shore. Nat takes a further risk by warning Brantley of the impending destruction; but, overjoyed at his salvation, Brantley hears nothing.

Nat's vision of contending black and white angels, his fasts and prayers, and his discoveries that white men were barely masters of themselves induce him to actuate his rebellion. Also, while working for the Whiteheads, Nat's hatred becomes so intensified that he lists it as a primary cause of his rebellion. Symptomatic of his split personal world is his ambivalent response to white kindness and his hatred of the white paternalistic system as he stands near Mrs. Whitehead:

Strange that, after a fashion, the woman's manner toward me had been ingratiating, even queerly tender, with a faint tongue-lick of unctuousness, benevolent, in a round-about way downright maternal. Nuzzling around my black ass. In my heart of hearts I bore her no ill will. Yet she had never once removed herself from the realm of ledgers, accounts, tallies, receipts, balance sheets, purse strings, profits, pelf—

as if the being to whom she was talking and around whom she had spun such a cocoon of fantasy had not been a creature with lips and fingernails and eyebrows and tonsils but some miraculous wheelbarrow. I gazed at the complacent oblong of her face, white as tallow. Suddenly I thought of the document beneath my shirt and again the hatred swept over me. I was seized with awe, and a realization: *Truly, that white flesh will soon be dead.* (327-28)

A provocative situation in which Margaret Whitehead, *en déshabille* and oblivious to Nat's feelings as a man, encounters him in the library only serves to frustrate and infuriate him further. In his feelings for Margaret, the unresolved love-hate relationship which Nat feels for whites is most intense. The effect of her naïve charms on Nat, puritan that he is, is maddening; and her antislavery feelings, as sincere as they are, do not offset his fevered response. Particularly Nat describes in a final idyllic scene the conflict between his libidinous and his messianic drives. Styron describes his feelings about such a scene in an interview:

The barrier is incredible, but it's tissue paper thin, and for just that reason it's all the more impermeable. And so the way that you break it down is in the most apocalyptic way that is possible to a human being. You break through it by killing. And it seems to me that this is symbolic of the human condition as we've experienced it in this country with the black and white races so incredibly on edge and so incredibly bound to each other. I don't want to set up a cliché. I don't want the usual black-man–white-man miscegenation nonsense. But I do think that there must have been a powerful thing at work here. I can't explain otherwise the fact that of all the people killed in the insurrection—all the white people; and there were sixty—that he should kill only one after trying, as he says himself in the confessions, to kill several and failing . . . why he should succeed with this one girl, an eighteen-year-old girl who's the only nubile girl, so far as I can find out, killed during the insurrection. So I think that this is a classic example of some sort of love-hate relationship.[22]

Nat gathers the nucleus of his forces in his Bible class. Though circumstances prevent Nat's original plan for a July Fourth rebellion, a series of rapid incidents quickens the pace of the novel toward the terrible violence of the rebellion. The accidental death of his master, Moore, brings him to the service of Mr. Travis, a loner from the mountains, with a "look and mood of the wilderness about him." Though Travis is a better master, Nat's determination and sense of mission become even stronger. Learning that there is to be a camp meeting in August which many whites will attend, Nat plans his rebellion for then. The attack begins at night on Travis's house. While the other slaves display the passions which rage in Nat, passions which drive them to physical violence, Nat himself cannot kill. Disturbed by his inability to strike Travis, he stands by while Will, insane with hatred, kills the white man:

I had laid my fingers on the haft of the ax again—dismayed at my irresolution and clumsiness, trembling in every bone—when there now took place that unforeseen act which would linger in my mind during whatever remaining days I was granted the power of memory. Just as I saw it happen I knew that it would be part of my being wherever I went, or whatever I was or became through my allotted time, even in the serene pastures of ancient age. For now as if from the outer dark, from nowhere, and with a silence that was a species of mystery in itself, Will hurled his body into the narrow space between myself and Travis, and his small black shape seemed to grow immense, somehow amorous, enveloping Travis's nightshirted figure in a brief embrace, almost as if he had joined him in a lascivious dance. (389)

Will's "dance" soon ends as his hatchet severs Travis's head at the neck while "Blood deluged the room in a foaming sacrament" (390). Will's hurtling attack derives from hatred of the "outer dark," a darkness to which Will had been thrust by the whites. It is not Nat's darkness, an introspective loneliness where love and need are as strong as hate and destruction; yet the image of the expanding black ball of hatred reflects his own rage at that moment.

The massacre continues as the rebellious slaves attack from other farms. Nat retains some control over his men, but the force of their attack and their success makes them less amenable to command. Drunkenness and lack of discipline weaken Nat's power over the men. By the time they arrive at Whitehead's, Nat's power is in question. Challenged by Will to prove himself, Nat pursues Margaret to her death.

Many of the murders are described in sexual terms. Will's "lascivious dance" with Travis is similar to his slaughter of Mrs. Whitehead: "Then I saw Will draw back as if from a kiss and with a swift sideways motion nearly decapitate Mrs. Whitehead in a single stroke" (412). Similarly, Nat's pursuit and attack on Margaret with his sword is a sexual encounter. As she tries to escape over a fence, the rotting poles give way; and "she tripped forward, bare arms still outthrust as if to welcome someone beloved and long unseen." Nat plunges his sword into her heart, but he has to club her to death to end her pain.

The rebellion continues and Nat retains control; but, with the death of Margaret, Nat's spirit and energy decline. Almost listlessly, he allows a young white girl to escape and to warn the community. Nat, who sees her disappear, says:

I might have reached her in a twinkling—the work of half a minute—but I suddenly felt dispirited and overcome by fatigue, and was pursued by an obscure, unshakable grief. I shivered in the knowledge of the futility of all ambition. My mouth was sour with the yellow recollection of death and blood-smeared fields and walls. I watched the girl slip away, vanish without a hand laid upon her. Who knows but whether we were not doomed to lose. I know nothing any longer. Nothing. Did I really wish to vouchsafe a life for the one that I had taken? (417)

XIV "Yet I Would Have Spared One"

Styron closes the novel in the prison where Nat awaits his execution. Nat dreams again of his voyage to the sea, past the promontory with the white temple; but, he cannot, he tells us, "dwell on that place too long, for again as always I know that to try to explore the mystery would be only to throw open portals on even deeper mysteries, on and on everlastingly, into the remotest corridors of thought and time" (422). Nat drifts in his dream to the sea, an even greater enigma. From an unknown source to an unforeseeable end, Nat is conveyed along by the boat's drift; and he moves toward "the arms of a steadfast and illimitable peace."

The morning star shines in the dawn of Nat's execution day. The brief incidents converge the themes of the novel and the significance of Nat's life: Gray's subdued tone and semirespect indicate that he has been affected by his encounter with Nat; Nat's cry against the savagery of the men who are tying Hark to the chair shows that Nat still rebels against their injustice; and, finally, the figure of Hark, carried "like the silhouette of some marvelous black potentate borne in stately procession toward his throne," shows Nat's sense of the essential dignity of the rebel. All these impressions build up to Nat's illusory union with Margaret:

Beloved, let us love one another: for love is of God; and everyone that loveth is borne of God, and knoweth God. Her voice is close, familiar, real, and for an instant I mistake the wind against my ear, a gentle gust, for her breath, and I turn to seek her in the darkness. And now beyond my fear, beyond my dread and emptiness, I feel the warmth flow into my loins and my legs tingle with desire. I tremble and I search for her face in my mind, seek her young body, yearning for her suddenly with a rage that racks me with a craving beyond pain; with tender stroking motions I pour out my love within her; pulsing flood, she arches against me, cries out, and the twain—black and white—are one. (426)

In Nat's autistic sexual union with Margaret, he physically identifies sexual and religious fulfillment. In so doing, he resolves the Oedipal conflict that has frustrated his relationship with all whites. Nat and Margaret were earlier united in her death by physical violence and hatred; in contrast, Nat is now redeemed in their sexual union of tenderness and love.[23]

That Margaret lacks the depth or awareness with which Nat invests her, that she is an illusory creation of his last moments, and that their "sexual union" is the result of Nat's masturbation affirm the ambiguity and the strength of Styron's close. Like Meursault in Camus's *The Stranger* or Yakov Bok in Malamud's novel *The Fixer*, the moment before death brings a sense not of resignation or defeat to these characters but one of rebellion and defiance. Meursault, who for the "first time" lays his "heart open to the benign indifference of the universe," despises the jeering crowd; Bok dreams of assassinating the czar. Through the *cause célèbre* of Bok's trial he has hastened the revolution and thus, like Meursault, has asserted himself. Nat has affirmed his manhood through rebellion and through his expression of love for Margaret. He has moved from isolation to self-discovery, which for all three of these novelists signifies redemption. Camus and Malamud make it clear that Meursault and Bok no longer need God; and, in a sense, Nat does not. He has discovered divinity in himself by breaking through the "barrier".

At the end, Nat has remorse only because of Margaret's death. In her sacrificial death and in his love for her he has been restored to human love: *"Yes, . . . I would have done it all again. I would have done it all again. I would have destroyed them all. Yet I would have spared one. I would have spared her that showed me Him whose presence I had not fathomed or maybe never even known. Great God, how early it is! Until now I had almost forgotten His name"* (428). Like Cordelia in *King Lear,* Margaret engenders love in a brutalized world. Nat Turner, who refuses the childlike role assigned him by the slave system, is called as God's child at the novel's end.

The Confessions of Nat Turner ends, like *Set This House on Fire,* on a note of redemption. Through his recollection of Margaret, Nat is redeemed by love, just as Cass is by self-purgation and murder. All of Styron's rebel-heroes share in the experience of an insight into their nature. Peyton admits to her incestuous passion, though it causes her suicide; Mannix discovers his limits as a man and that the rage for freedom can turn a rebel into a tyrant; Cass, on the other hand, goes beyond the limits of guilt and childish self-pity, which he imposes on himself, to move gradually toward maturity. In each of the earlier novels, a sympathetic observer is involved, but not in the *Confessions.* For Nat connects with no man really, except Margaret. Of enemies who represent the institutionalized world, Nat has plenty; but there is no sympathetic observer whose viewpoint gives another angle of vision on the main character.

The effect of this single point of view is to emphasize Nat's isolation and his self-containment. Nat is not caught in a childish rebellion but in one legitimately involved with freedom to be a man, not a child. If he loses his humanity in the course of that rebellion and destroys Margaret, he also regains through her sacrifice his ability to love as a man. Most important, Nat lives through his own strength; therefore, we see him through his perspective alone.

The Confessions of Nat Turner has already evoked critical comparisons with other southern writers, and some validity exists in this point of view. Yet Styron, like his predecessor, Faulkner, goes beyond regional limitations in his novel; but, unlike Faulkner, Styron is absorbed with the condition of the rebel. Rebellion even in its failure is preferable to "endurance." None of these considerations can be ignored in Styron's work; they are what make him an accomplished artist.

CHAPTER 6

Satire, Psychology, and Social Issues

The Confessions of Nat Turner is Styron's most successful characterization of his rebel-hero, but the earlier novels are indicative of that other objective which Styron pursues in his fiction: the condemnation of what is false in modern life. As in the case of his earlier heroes, Peyton, Mannix, and Cass, the social environment affects the rebel's character and his act of rebellion against the system. Peyton is promiscuous in a society of loveless sex; Mannix, in his madness, becomes a super-marine martinet; Cass is sickeningly childish in a society which encourages immediate gratification; and Nat Turner becomes partially brutalized by a corrupt and violent system.

I Satire in Styron's Novels

In the earlier novels Styron regards and describes the environment satirically as well as apocalyptically. We are reminded of the description of Peyton's wedding party, of Mason's film people, or of the absurd situations of Mannix and Cass when they rant against the system to which, ironically, they unconsciously subscribe. But there is little satire in *The Confessions of Nat Turner*. Nat Turner, like Peyton, Mannix, and Cass, is turned toward violence by the system; and, through violence and suffering, he arrives at a recognition by the end of the novel. Though there are ironies in Nat's encounters with the surrounding society, there are relatively few comic or absurd situations. Simply and specifically, we view all incidents through Nat's consciousness, which is that of a man who is trying to achieve manhood within a social system which insists on his remaining a child.

Styron's interest in satire in *Lie Down in Darkness* and in *Set This House on Fire* is also manifested in two reviews. One of them, written in 1961 about Mrs. Aadland's *The Big Love*, is an account of Beverly Aadland's incredible amours with Errol Flynn; the second is a review of Terry Southern's *Candy*. In the first of these reviews, Styron, aided by the ridiculous incongruities of Flo's and Beverly's account of Beverly's affair with the movie star, has a field day with an "unintentionally comic masterpiece." It is a book which, Styron says, "in a grotesque fashion surpasses all aesthetic laws."

Significantly, *Big Love* suggests to Styron Nathanael West's *Day of the Locust*, "if for no other reason than the fact that, as in that fine and funny book, in which horror and laughter are commingled like the beginning of a scream, the climax of *Big Love* plunges toward nightmare and hallucination in a fashion which all but overwhelms the comedy." [1] The grotesqueries of the situations recall Styron's belief that "only a great satirist can tackle the world's problems and articulate them." [2] Styron's ideas about this subject are shared by a number of contemporary writers who have expressed similar views in essays on fiction. [3] How Styron himself employs satire and parody is most evident in Cass's characterization as well as in Styron's description of the environment in *Set This House on Fire*.

Styron regards Terry Southern's novel, *Candy,* as a satire on bad pornography. To Styron, pornography "causes disgust" in the reader; and the most pornographic books are those of "mechanical howtoism, with its clubfooted prose and its desolating veterinary odor. . . . Those books . . . constitute the really prurient writing of our time." The real evil is that they reduce sexual love, as Mason Flagg and his group in *Set This House on Fire* do, to a test of skill rather than making it a human expression of honest emotions. "Candy's seducers," continues Styron, "are technocrats and experts, possessing a lust to bury this most fundamental of human impulses beneath the rockpile of scientific paraphernalia and doctrine and professional jabber." [4] In Styron's view, *Candy* is a valuable satire on the contemporary sexual scene; but his review has even greater importance because of the values he implies in the nature of sexuality as an expression of personality.

II Styron and Sexuality

In *Set This House on Fire*, Mason Flagg is the voice of the new sexual frontier; but his sexual adventures and supposed prowess are revealed as the impotent gestures of a man wholly incapable of love. Yet Styron uses sexuality as a form of bodily expression in his fiction, as a correlative physical experience which reflects the tortured feelings of his characters. Peyton's promiscuity in *Lie Down in Darkness* is a sexual manifestation not only of her rebellion against her mother's puritanical standards but also of an expression of her love-hate relationship with her father. None of her sexual encounters are described with any joy on her part; they are expressions of revenge against her father or Harry for their failures as father-lovers. Sex for Peyton is a tortured, painful experience, impossible of fulfillment. In *Set This House on Fire*, Cass's sexual encounters match his mental struggles; the episode with the girl evangelist reflects his sense of waste and naïveté. Sex in that novel belongs within the "technical" domain of Mason Flagg and is, therefore, more the subject of satire.

In *The Confessions of Nat Turner*, sexuality plays a major role as an expression of Turner's isolation and loneliness. Though several critics have pointed out that Nat Turner had a wife in fact,[5] Styron chose to make him "a celibate because [Turner] seemed to have the single-minded, ascetic character you often find in revolutionary figures." [6] It should be added that, in creating his fictional version of Nat Turner, Styron presents a strong psychological case for Nat Turner's sexual composition. From his childhood on, Nat Turner associates sex with violence and betrayal, as in the brutal rape of his mother by the white overseer, or in Miss Emmeline's tryst with her lover. Only in sexual fantasy, in masturbation, or in his homosexual experience with Willis does Nat Turner find an outlet from the system and its restrictions. His sexual experiences, like those of his mind, separate him from other men; but Nat Turner is not incapable of desire or feeling for others. He is not permitted under the system to express those feelings, and his frustration, resulting from acceptance and then from rejection, is ultimately a strong basis for his rebellion.

III Religious Attitudes in Styron's Works

Sexual love is inextricably connected with religious feeling in Styron's novels. In *Lie Down in Darkness*, the three Loftises, because of their relation to their individual fathers, fail to see sexual love as an adult relationship. Helen's father image is that of a Puritan father-God of Wrath; and neither Milton nor Cary, the minister, fulfills her concept of a redeemer since neither views sex with anything like her Puritan abhorrence. Milton uses sex as a revenge against Helen's moralistic self-righteousness, and his adultery with Dolly is his rather banal rebellion against Helen's Puritanism and her castrating self-righteousness. Peyton's misuse of sex grows out of the lessons learned from her parents —contempt for men and revenge through adultery.

The inability of these people to love is the heritage and the curse of a Puritan-Romantic society. Religion is dead because sexual love is dead. Lying down in darkness does not only relate to the quotation from Sir Thomas Browne's *Hydriotaphia: Urn-Burial* which heralds the novel. Styron, by repeating the phrase throughout the novel, evokes the contemplation of death, the vanity of the world, and the hope of Christian immortality. But he also attaches the phrase to the death of sexual love and to the failure of the characters to see or know one another as lovers.

Religion and sexual love are also intimately related in *Set This House on Fire*. The opening quotation from Donne's sermon, with its sexual imagery of God's trying to force a way into man's "house" and with its reminder of the sonnet "Batter my heart three-personed God," is carried through in the violent action of the novel. Hell, to Donne, is when God has excluded him "as though I had cost him nothing, that this God at last, should let this soule goe away . . . [and it] must *lie in darknesse*" (italics mine). The coincidence of phrase found in Styron's novel and in Donne is not accidental. Styron means that lying in darkness is total abandonment by God; and, for Cass in *Set This House on Fire*, that abandonment is the waste of spirit, the "divine spirit" that flows out of him in the central episode with the girl evangelist. Instead of waste of spirit, man must rage and burn; and he must set his house on fire in passion, anger, and finally violence. This purgation rids Cass of the twin evils of Romantic egoism and Puritan guilt. In that moment in the novel when Cass, lying naked and alone in darkness after a pointless "sinister Lethean romp," can shriek, "Dio non esiste !," the idea of loveless sex (like Flagg's mechanical sex) is linked with the death of God.

Similarly, in *The Confessions of Nat Turner*, sexual fulfillment, autoerotic or otherwise, is directly connected with religion or religious feelings. This relationship is particularly significant at the end of *The Confessions of Nat Turner* where Nat Turner's sexual fulfillment and his love for Margaret are fused in his religious experience[7] and where his language is reminiscent of the Song of Solomon. Though sexual love in *The Confessions of Nat Turner* can be a gentle and redeeming force, sexual violence often expresses the frustrations, hatreds, and fears that Nat experiences.

IV Styron's Use of Violence

The use of violence in Styron's fiction is characteristically associated with the very nature of rebellion. Peyton Loftis commits violence against her body and ends in suicide; Mannix tortures his men and himself; and Cass Kinsolving wastes and murders. The rebel hero's violence is generally directed at the system, but invariably the force of his violence is centered on one particular representative. In each novel the rebels, and the forms and objects of their violence, naturally vary; but the violence is a necessary preliminary to self-discovery and redemption. As in Dostoevski's *The Brothers Karamazov,* the worst and most violent sinners against men are often capable of self-awareness and sainthood.

In *The Confessions of Nat Turner,* the system gives its promise of freedom; but its reality of violence is slavery. In the earlier fiction, the system is shown in representative incidents and in representative characters (Helen, Templeton, or Flagg). But in *The Confessions of Nat Turner* the system is seen through a number of representative characters, including Gray, Cobb, Samuel Turner, and Margaret, who display a range of degree in responsibility. Gray is a fairly unambiguous villain, but Samuel Turner's villainy is more serious because he promises freedom. Ultimately, Nat Turner may regret Margaret's death; but, when he kills her, he has reached a point where, like Peyton, Mannix, and Cass, there is no other way to "break down" the barrier except through violence to himself or to others. I do not imply that, in *The Confessions of Nat Turner,* Styron is advocating violence, but that he is presenting the psychological conditions which precede violence: the promise given and never fulfilled; the violence given and returned in kind.

The contiguity of violence to sexual and religious matters is not only an outgrowth of Styron's use of the Bible as a source for his imagery, but also an indication of his awareness of the powerful sexual currents in the Old Testament. Nat Turner, to Styron, was a religious esthetic, and his dedication to revolution has its roots in his strong religious sentiments. Styron, in one of his interviews, speaks not only of Turner's sense of being "chosen" but also of his assumption of "heroic proportions." [8] He was able to revolt because he was not of the plantation-slave system; therefore, he was not totally "brutalized spiritually," as were most other slaves.

Yet the system has had its effect upon him through the acceptance-rejection pattern, a pattern denied to the other slaves in the novel; and the effect of this pattern impels him toward active rebellion. For, as John Hope Franklin says in defining the main theme of *The Confessions of Nat Turner,* "Freedom cannot be compromised, nor can it be meted out as though it were crumbs from a bountiful table." [9]

V The Controversy Over the Confessions

Throughout this study I have been viewing this particular novel primarily as a work of literature, but it is also a social document. Styron has recognized and is obviously prepared to face the consequences of the novel's interpretation as a comment on revolution, past and current. The preface to the novel and the fact that he has publicly appeared to defend his book indicate that he felt a need to clarify his objectives. I believe he did so to emphasize the imaginative, speculative elements in his novel and the basic fact that a good deal of himself had gone into Nat Turner's characterization. This clarification was necessary because most contemporary readers might have regarded the novel as primarily an historical document rather than as fiction.

Despite, or in some cases because of, Styron's prefatory remarks, several critics have drawn attention to Styron's alteration of some of the historical details. The planned film of the novel by Wolpert Pictures, Ltd., which bought the screen rights for six hundred thousand dollars, has already involved the National Association for the Advancement of Colored People. The assistant executive director of that organization, John

Morselli, stated that it planned a "presentation" to insure that "offensive aspects are purged from the movie." [10]

The most strident response to the novel is, however, a collection of essays by black writers, *William Styron's Nat Turner: Ten Black Writers Respond,* edited by John Clark, an editor of *Freedom Ways.*[11] The ten writers share a view of literature as a vehicle for "history" and also the conviction that Aptheker's thesis about slave revolts is so totally valid that it does not allow for other literary or historical presentations of that past. The fact that Styron is a white Southerner provides a basis for criticizing his novel, as well as his predilection toward a psychological approach to Nat Turner's life. On this basis, all of the writers insist on the premeditated plan of Styron to write a racist tract designed to praise the slave system; to regenerate black stereotypes; and, in general, to comfort the white middle class by assuaging its guilt and responsibility. In a review of the essays in the *New York Review of Books,*[12] Eugene Genovese has pointed out the historical relevancy and accuracy of Styron's fictional presentation of a black leader and the slave system against which he rebelled. Given the limited knowledge of Nat Turner's personality, Styron presents a sensitive, complex, and human character that emphasizes his virtues and his ability to extend himself to others.

In his review, Genovese answers the major questions raised by the essayists about the social content of the novel; and he emphasizes the need to understand the "antagonistic qualities" which "appear at the same moment and in the same men." The questions raised by other reflections on history, such as Hannah Arendt's *Eichmann in Jerusalem,* are related to Styron's attempt in this novel to reflect the mood and temperament of human beings caught in a soul-destroying system. The reaction of many Jews to Hannah Arendt's less than heroic portrayal of concentration-camp prisoners parallels the response of the essayists in this collection to the picture of the slaves' lives. They fail to see that the system must be seen in all its nihilistic horror for it to be really understood by contemporary readers.

Not all Negro critics agree, however, about the significance of the novel. Dr. John Hope Franklin, Chairman of the History Department of the University of Chicago, when defending the novel in the *San Francisco Chronicle* of March 19, 1968, says: "I thought it was a great book. . . . In his meditation Styron makes many salient comments and observations that reveal his profound understanding of the institution of slavery." [13]

The attack on Styron from both sides in the contemporary clash over race in America was expected. James Baldwin, who considers *The Confessions of Nat Turner* as the beginning of a "common history—ours," is cognizant of Styron's risks in writing the novel. Styron, by fictionalizing history through his own experience and through psychological identification with Nat Turner, is working in the way he believes most effective for freeing both black and white men from the trap of racial blindness. Baldwin, who acted as a "catalyst" for Styron in dissolving some of the obstacles which kept Styron from "seeing" Nat Turner, feels the novel is a "troubling book":

Styron is probing something very dangerous, deep and painful in the national psyche. I hope it starts a tremendous fight, so that people will learn what they really think about each other.

It'll be called effrontery . . . but it isn't that. It's a very courageous book that attempts to fuse the two points of view, the master's and the slave's. In that sense the book is hopeful. It's important for the black reader to see what Bill is trying to do and to recognize its validity.[14]

The controversy over the novel received more attention after an appearance by Styron at Smith College on February 10, 1968, during which he offered a "point-by-point defense" of his book against criticism. To Styron, the discrepancies of historical fact in his novel are understandable because he aims at some larger truth involved in Nat Turner's portrayal as a fictional character. Comparison with George Bernard Shaw's *St. Joan,* Bertolt Brecht's *Galileo,* or John Osborne's *Luther* shows that creative artists can fictionalize or even fantasize the lives of historical personages to portray what they consider to be an essential truth about these men. This attitude toward the historical personages draws some support from writers like Norman O. Brown (*Life Against Death: The Psychoanalytical Meaning of History*) and Erik H. Erikson (*Young Man Luther,* a psychoanalytical-historical study of emerging leadership).

Styron's novel is a "meditation on history." It was the particular striking historical fact that Margaret Whitehead was the only person killed by Turner that attracted Styron, and he made this a basis for his fictional treatment of Nat Turner's psychological development and attitude toward women. Styron's view about the use and misuse of love in *The Confessions of Nat Turner* compares significantly with his attitudes toward the erotic in his earlier fiction. For, if we consider the manner in which Styron views sexual relationships in his fiction, and his use of psychologically motivated violence, Nat Turner's actions in the novel are justified. None of the historical accounts, sympathetic or not, including Drewry and Aptheker[15] whom Styron consulted, explain Turner's single murder. Intrigued by this fact, Styron created Nat Turner by psychologically identifying with the slave's frustrations, rage, and violence (even to the point of having Nat Turner lose his mother at the age of thirteen, the same age that Styron lost his), and with the images of the white parent figures who often simultaneously encourage and thwart his struggle to be free.

To say, as one critic has, that *The Confessions of Nat Turner* is a "racist book designed to titillate the fantasies of white America," [16] is to misread not only Styron's accounts of sexuality but also the acceptance-rejection pattern of his character's life. That pattern creates in the fictional Nat Turner his spiritual isolation, his rage, and his love, as it would in the sexual lives of most men subjected to such a system. Nor is the novel meant to "comfort" white "middlebrow" readers. Instead, Styron makes Nat Turner's anger comprehensible through the acceptance-rejection experiences of his life.

Styron's best defense lies in a careful reading of his novel, a reading which takes into consideration his use of sex and violence, as well as the means and causes for his development of Turner's character. Most important, it must be viewed as presenting a truth about men in revolution through fiction. This truth about revolutionary change is one of Styron's concerns; he wants to awaken an historical sense in Americans of what is taking place in the world. In his interview with James Jones, he said: "We have never recognized until recently that the obvious stream of history could be in a great measure the story of what happens when X million Africans rise up and assert

themselves. The story of Nat Turner is a little microcosmic—
a thing which took place *here,* but which represents to me the
whole continent of Africa.[17]

Nat Turner's rebellion is connected with the revolutionary
movements so perceptively described in Franz Fanon's *The
Wretched of the Earth.*[18] His discussion of the revolutionary
movements of former colonial peoples against imperialism is
relevant to the racism inherent in American society which permitted slavery before the Civil War and which continued
economic, political, and social bondage of black men after it.
In this respect, Styron, as a Southerner, is as acutely conscious
of the existence of racism with all its psychological and social
ambiguities in white America as are many Northern liberals
who have rested secure by hating the Ku Klux Klan and by
supporting the National Association for the Advancement of
Colored People. For white America, Styron's book not only
means the sharing of guilt for an indigenous colonialism and the
obligation to escape the "back water of history" that has separated us from the reality of the revolutionary currents of
contemporary history; it also demands a commitment from the
reader to understand the mental frustrations and emotional
crises of the black rebel's mind.

For Styron, *The Confessions of Nat Turner* involved a personal confrontation with the failure and the guilt of the American
past as well as a psychological identity with the black victims
of that heritage.

CHAPTER 7

Styron and the South

Styron, in writing *The Confessions of Nat Turner,* felt a need to return to his Southern past to probe the moral predicament of the present, just as earlier writers, like Faulkner and Robert Penn Warren, did. Styron, however, has a viewpoint which differs markedly from these two earlier writers. In Faulkner's best work, the sense of doom, of people chained to a guilt from a time past, is evident; in Warren, the desire for order, for an ethos of responsibility for guilt, is central to his work. In Styron, the motif is of individual rage and rebellion—and as assertion of humanity as a means of atonement for guilt in the midst of chaos.

The development in these three Southern writers is indicative of a change in Southern life, but it reflects also the break with the past of Western civilization of the twentieth century. In fact, much of the national and international interest in both Faulkner and Warren has been based on their moral concern about a society of rapidly changing values. Continuing in that tradition, Styron's work has generated a similar interest.[1] There is much that marks his work as part of the "Southern" school beyond the geographical. Styron has a tendency toward symbol and allegory, particularly in *Set This House on Fire,* though his inclinations are not so strong as Faulkner's in *Light in August* or in *Absalom, Absalom!* The disposition to employ symbol and allegory is something viewed as a hallmark of the Southern school of writing, though quite clearly it is prevalent in much nineteenth-century American fiction.

From the first, critics who have recognized the quality of Styron's work have identified him as a Southern writer. Styron, like Faulkner, has endeavored, I believe with some success, to free himself from this regional limitation. Although the two narrators in *Set This House on Fire*—Peter, who tends to associate himself with the Tidewater gentleman, and Cass, the Carolina hill man—indicate Styron's double view of the changes in Southern society, his perspective ranges far wider. In this respect, it is necessary to compare Styron with other writers who work in a Southern setting and to clarify this regional relationship.

In several ways Southern fiction resulting from the "Southern experience" has had certain critical hallmarks that have ostensibly given it distinction from other American writing. The Southern "experience" after the Civil War was never associated with the expanding economy of the North and the West, nor with the success and invincibility of American national and international standing nor, for that matter, with the overweening optimism of American life. Most significant was the lack in Southern literature of Whitmanian or Emersonian optimism, an abstraction of time and space that opens to the future.

Instead, Southern writers have often turned to historical consciousness of the past as it exists in the present. They sometimes share with some non-Southern American writers of the post-World War I society (Hemingway, Cather, Anderson) a Twainian nostalgia for a lost and simpler past. Although this past life was corrupted by life along the shore in *Huckleberry Finn* and by the double sin of human and territorial bondage in *The Bear*, both Twain and Faulkner prefer the past to the decline of values, the destruction of nature, the mechanical evils, and the resultant society of the present. Faulkner's work heralds and criticizes the New South, one whose "experience" inexorably is becoming indistinguishable from the rest of the nation; and Warren's and Styron's novels deal with the actualities of that situation.

The South is presently involved in a social and economic revolution which has already leveled many of the landmarks of regional distinctiveness and which has the additional support of a moral judgment directed against a pillar of the traditional past—segregation. Even a sentimentalist would have to admit the material advantages of Southern progress; and, if any one were to condemn the South for faults and weaknesses, it would be for blemishes which appear today to be less Southern and more American in character. There have been, however, two attempts to hold on to Southern tradition which have met with varied lack of success. For the first attempt, by the Agrarians of the Fugitive group in the 1930's, it was clear that their belief in the preservation of humanist culture was not shared by most Southerners who found the appeal of industrial capitalism far stronger.

The second attempt by diehard segregationists was to argue that the ultimate test of Southern unity, its "central theme," was racial consciousness and white supremacy. This second argument has had more political success than those of the Southern Agrarians, but it is obvious that this attempt to sustain a "regional" tradition will also fail for moral or economic reasons. Primarily, the "tradition" fails because it requires the subservience of the black man in order to continue; and such servitude is no longer possible morally or politically. Secondly, the South, like former agricultural regions that have become industrialized, in manners and customs and to a great extent in physical appearance, assumes the surface homogeneity of modern urban life, a condition which makes the continuance of the harmful myth of plantation life impossible to maintain. The accompanying breakdown of community, the destruction of the myths and traditions which bind it together, the uprooting of individuals, and the tendency toward conformity and toward that nebulous goal of the "American Way of Life" are marks of the changes taking place in the South.[2]

I   The Changing Attitude of Southern Writers: Faulkner, Warren, and Styron

After World War I the Southern writer slowly began to separate from his community and from the daily existence of his fellow Southerners. He began to create out of his own reality another and larger reality than the life around him. Faulkner's work exemplifies this shift from community to personal values and the losses involved. Much of Faulkner's work directly concerns the gradual collapse of the community and implies the need for the writer to outgrow that community in order to explore its sickness.

For Faulkner, the compounded sin of slavery of people and land remains unabsolved; nor can the community ever be really cleansed of these sins. The persistence of doom seen in Sutpen's debacle and in the Compsons' decline is countered only by Faulkner's primitives who "endure." But Dilsey, Lena Grove, and the Bundrens belong to another time; and, though they are possessed with a greater inner strength than the Christians, Ike McCaslin, Byron Bunch, and Hightower, they too are ineffectual against fate. Faulkner's fictional world now belongs to the unethical, materialistic Snopses, and it becomes, in the end, a subject for satire.

Faulkner's fatalistic sense has its roots in the Southern version of original sin, the bondage of men and land. His sense of doom is based on the impossibility of a return to Eden, and the tragedy of man lies in this impossibility. Faulkner traces this moral decline in Sutpen in *Absalom, Absalom!* from the fall from a free primitive community of hill people to the corrupted plantation society. There is no return possible for Sutpen to the land of primitive tranquillity.

Wright Morris in "The Territory Ahead" [3] describes the phenomena of Faulkner's rage and violence which lie at the opposite pole to his "mythic peace," and Morris explains why this polarity no longer has meaning for many contemporary writers. It lacks significance primarily because the illusory world of the mythic past can prevent man from confronting his present reality.

Polarization of order and violence of another kind than Faulkner's is present in the fiction of Warren. In Faulkner, the tragic note cannot be struck without a positive world order; but for Warren this order lies in the concept of an ordered society, not in a nostalgia for a primitive past. His novels are concerned with political and economic struggles of men as these are seen through psychological and moral perspective. Set against violence is order, and order means living by principles. In Warren's novels the psychological discipline of the principled man is totality and balance between reason and passion, and he moves within a framework of traditional humanistic society and religious values.

Twain, Faulkner, and Warren are generally identified as American writers who have their cultural roots at least partially if not wholly in the American South. Styron, too, recognizes his debt to the past which gave him "an enormous sense of tradition . . . family, community, place." [4] But he is also aware that the frameworks which were operable for Faulkner and Warren are illusory today and that the struggle is relegated to an individual's self-confrontation and self-redemption.

In an interview early in his career, Styron spoke of his desire to escape the limitations of a regional outlook in his novels without sacrificing some of the advantages of the tragic heritage of the South: "I wanted to write a novel that has more than regional implications. I wanted to avoid the ancestral theme, too—the peculiar inbred and perverse types that Faulkner, Caldwell, and other Southern writers have dealt in. At the same time I didn't want to exploit the old idea of wreckage and defeat as a peculiarly Southern phenomenon." [5] Three years later Styron was still emphasizing this point in the interview for the *Paris Review* when he said that "Only certain things in the book [*Lie Down in Darkness*] are particularly Southern . . . I would like to believe that my people would have behaved the way they did anywhere." [6]

John Aldridge, who reviewed *Lie Down in Darkness* for the *New York Times,* argued that Styron is mistaken: "the Southern elements of the novel—particularly the elements of fundamentalist religion, regionalist guilt, and the contrast of races—are, in fact, so powerful that, if anything, they seem excessive to the motives of the characters and perpetually to overpower them." [7] Another critic, F. J. Hoffman, referring to *Lie Down in Darkness,* took a slightly different tack: "While this novel cannot be called 'Southern' in its use of setting, its central concern is the loss of that rapport that has been celebrated or defended in other novels of its place and time." [8]

Malcolm Cowley's praiseworthy review of *Lie Down in Darkness,* entitled "The Faulkner Pattern," [9] set the tone for most of the early evaluations of Styron. Cowley expended most of his critical energy praising Styron for using the material of Faulkner's *As I Lay Dying* and, even more, that of *The Sound and the Fury.* Styron's book, he wrote, was an exception to the rule that "novels which stay close to their literary models have no great value of their own." Indeed, Cowley becomes so absorbed in the superficial similarities of plot and character as to cite Peyton's suicide scene as an improvement over Quentin's; but he misses the basic differences in character, setting, and theme between Faulkner's novel and Styron's.

Because of this critical identification, Styron has been considered as a Southern novelist—as one whose viewpoint is determined primarily by regional considerations. Yet not all critics have been easy either in their labeling of Styron as a regional writer or in their identifying him with Faulkner. Walter Sullivan, for instance, points out how imitative William Humphrey is of Faulkner in *Home from the Hill* as opposed to Styron's different viewpoint. "What is most significant about Styron as a Southerner is that, unlike many of his predecessors, he seems to be more or less at home in the modern world." [10]

Louis Rubin presents the clearest statement of Styron's differences from earlier Southern writers. In his study of writers in the modern South, *The Faraway Country*,[11] Rubin uses the literature of the period as a reflection of Southern life. Tracing the roots of contemporary Southern writers through the Genteel Southern literary tradition and the literary generation of the 1920's and 1930's, Rubin concludes that Styron's work represents several noteworthy changes in the character of Southern writing. Southern literature of the Genteel period was not a literature of exiles spiritually alienated from their community; it was rooted in the manners, customs, and sense of community. This community, despite its failures and superficialities, provided the spiritual and moral needs as well as the guilt and responsibility for the writer. Rubin's analysis explains Styron's desire to use the Southern past without becoming nostalgically involved in it.

Styron's viewpoint developed partly out of his literary heritage and particularly from Faulkner and Warren. The social and economic changes were recorded and commented on by both those writers, but Styron differs from them by not looking back and by presenting lives of men—in an Existential framework of confrontation with their own lives; lives are not presented in a framework of past guilt and doom or even of social responsibility.

II Styron and Camus

In the same interview for the *Red Clay Reader* in which Styron stated his debt to his Southern heritage, he remarked that the Southern influence is there "only in the sense that a tradition of Southern writing has been more or less important in forming me as a writer . . . much of my experience has been formed from other backgrounds—the North, Europe." [12] By Europe, Styron particularly means France; for, in a letter to Pierre Brodin in 1963, Styron explicitly described his debt to French literature:

I learned what real "writing" was, and Flaubert was a determining influence in my style. I faithfully re-read Flaubert every two or three years. Of the moderns of any nationality, including the United States, Camus has had the largest effect upon my thinking, and I have valued the quality of his moral intensity more than anything I have found in any other contemporary. Consequently, I believe certain French attitudes have entered my writing, and last year in Paris—where, to my agreeable surprise, my last book was greeted with such enthusiasm by French readers—I could not help but be pleased when I was told by an eminent critic that it was hard for him to believe that I was not French. [13]

Particularly in *Set This House on Fire* and in *The Confessions of Nat Turner* we have seen the influence of Camus. This European influence distinguishes Styron's viewpoint from that of his Southern predecessors and, as in the case of two of his contemporaries in American fiction, Bellow and Hawkes, gives an Existential cast to his work. Styron's world is one of despair; and, like these American writers, he puts his despair to constructive use.

III   Styron's Creative Despair

Influenced by French writers and philosophers, Styron has taken his fiction beyond the limits of a traditional or primitive past and has entered into a situation where tragedy is no longer feasible. The contemporary writer, says Wright Morris, does not fear extinction so much as the "prescient chill of heart of a world without consciousness." [14] Styron shows us some of its results in *Lie Down in Darkness*. In that novel the failure of traditional and primitive values brings the Loftises to the abyss of despair. In his three other novels, however, Styron's characters achieve a recognition of themselves. They arrive at identity without reliance on the past but through rebellion and the subsequent sense of their limitations.

We cannot say that the Southern setting and the sense of

tragic doom contribute to the actions of the characters even in *Lie Down in Darkness*. In that novel the major conflicts and tensions result from domestic tragedy, or from a heightening of the basic struggles that are in the nature of family life. Milton's immaturity and visionary dreams of glory and Helen's nostalgic adulation of preadolescence are characteristic in extreme of many American marriages. Though primarily caused by her guilt over her incestuous child love, Peyton's suicide is partly the result of her parents' unrelenting war. Again, though the Southern setting is less significant than the American atmosphere of a changing wartime society and the atomic bomb, both are necessary background to the basic family struggle. Within Styron's imagination, the descriptions of the events in the family's life are juxtaposed with events in the world as a way of elevating family tragedy to a higher level. His model remains essentially the Greek tragic drama, but without the cosmic ramifications of that drama. Finally, and most significantly, there is continual emergence and examination of the rebel figure in Styron's fiction, a subject which is not limited to a particular time or place but to a man's conflict with a system which binds and cripples him.

Wright Morris, in speaking of the modern temper, speaks directly to the subject of moral and creative energies; and he calls our attention to the new view of man and to his tragic-absurd condition:

If the modern temper, as distinct from the romantic, lies in the admission that men are mortal, this admission determines the nature of the raw material with which the artist must work. An element of despair, a destructive element, is one of the signs by which we shall know him—the other is the constructive use to which this element is put. It distinguishes this artist from the seriously hopeful, or the hopefully serious, who cannot bring themselves to admit of the contemporary facts. These men *know* better, almost without exception, but their hope lies in the refusal to admit what they know. This common failure of admission characterizes their work and blights their hope. The modern temper finds its facts, and its hope, in the statement by Albert Camus: "I want to know if I can live with what I know and only with that." [15]

Essentially, it is for this "knowledge" that Styron's heroes strive and achieve. In an early essay, Styron presents the most important theme of his work by attacking the "easy optimism which arises not so much from revulsion against prevailing literary patterns of darkness and despair as from a lack of perspective." [16] Citing Euripides, Dante, and Shakespeare as proof that great art is born of a pessimistic view of life and that one must nurture hope through infinite despair, Styron began and continues to write in the belief that it is better to have writers pass through the horror of decay and hopelessness than to turn to an early gratuitous optimism. Indeed, the passage through defeat and despair is the ordeal of all of the rebellious protagonists of Styron's novels; and this progression is evident in his work from *Lie Down in Darkness* to *The Confessions of Nat Turner*. He remains consistent in his view that the vision of the abyss of suffering is the beginning of wisdom. But such wisdom is the sense of identity, the re-creation of self.

In Styron's work, he is primarily concerned with the tragic condition of man's ancient feud with his own nature and destiny. Rather than show man as the product of an environment of ancestral guilt and doom against which he heroically casts himself, Styron allows his characters (including the Loftises in *Lie Down in Darkness*) that freedom of choice to continually struggle against their self-indulgent and self-destructive urge to lie down in darkness. The confrontation with self in that novel is, at the very least, the beginning of a tragic awareness that man's greatest enemy lies in himself. In Styron's developing view, the three later novels end not in doom or in redemption but in an awareness that simultaneously and paradoxically includes both an acknowledgment of suffering and death as well as a redemption.

The act of rebellion in Styron's novels is, in summary, a rejection at first of a deterministic system through the awareness and affirmation the hero has of his own nature. In the course of this rebellion, he exorcises the evils of the system in himself and breaks through the barriers to his own self-awareness through violence to himself or others. The violence is a necessary concomitant to the vision of the abyss of nothingness which opens up for each of Styron's characters and which for each is the beginning of awareness. From this acknowledgment, each character moves toward his redemption.

Accompanying the journeys toward self-discovery of the Loftises, Mannix and Culver, or the journeys of redemption and renewal of Cass Kinsolving and Nat Turner are the descriptive passages, the creations of Styron's poetic vision. We have seen in the first three novels how the stream of consciousness and symbolic description in *Lie Down in Darkness,* the juxtaposing images in *The Long March* and the hyperbole in *Set This House on Fire* add to the levels of consciousness and meaning in these novels. In *Lie Down in Darkness,* Peyton's poetic soliloquy draws together all the disparate points of view of the novel, the imagery of flightless birds and womb-clocks underscores the futility of the Loftises' lives. Or again in *The Long March,* Styron uses the juxtaposition of metal and human parts scattered after the mortar explosion to symbolically enlarge his atmosphere of violence and rebellion. *Set This House on Fire* provides even more numerous examples, as we have seen, of Styron's descriptive prose, with the distinction that it is narrated in the first person and at times even parodies itself. All of these examples demonstrate Styron's development, culminating in his creation of the voice of Nat Turner, with his biblical phrasing and poetic vision of destruction and creation in the last sequence of *The Confession of Nat Turner.*

A vision of the destructive abyss is given to each of Styron's major characters in the four novels. For Peyton in *Lie Down in Darkness,* the reality of her situation is too horrible to confront; and she destroys herself. At the end of her life she comprehends though she cannot redeem herself. This same self-destructive tendency is demonstrable in Mannix of *The Long March,* in Cass Kinsolving of *Set This House on Fire,* and in Nat Turner of *The Confessions of Nat Turner* in the rebellions which they perpetrate. Paradoxically, the justice of their causes, or their success or failure, is secondary to the fact that they all attain a new evaluation of themselves. Such recognition of self is the true central theme of all of Styron's work, and it is presented through his settings and what I call his "double perspective." It is not a tragic recognition in the Classical sense, for that would imply an order or framework larger than the personal experience. It is rather a confrontation with a personal reality, an identification of self stripped of all illusions and aware of its human limitations.

Styron's heroes are like Lear on the heath; but, where Shakespeare's Lear had broken the "natural order," Styron's people have no order of reference except themselves and must consequently create their own values. The minds of Styron's rebels, if they wish to remain alive, must continually return to the sources of rebellion and draw energy from the awareness that recognizes limits. In that sense, their lives become a continuous act of rebellion. After Oedipus's or Lear's tragic recognition, there is acceptance—an affirmation of the place of man in the cosmos. But, for Styron's Existential heroes, their recognition signals the beginning of their struggle. They often fail, as we would expect; but their continued rebellion is as necessary as breathing is to them. In their depiction and in the poetic imagination which elevates their struggle, Styron achieves his artistic triumph.

Notes and References

Chapter One

1. Malcolm Cowley, "The Faulkner Pattern," *New Republic*, CXXV (October 8, 1951), 19-20. Review of *Lie Down in Darkness*. Alfred Kazin, "Instinct for Tragedy," *Book World, Chicago Tribune* (October 8, 1967), 1, 22. Review of *The Confessions of Nat Turner*.

2. John W. Aldridge, *After the Lost Generation* (New York, 1951), discusses the failure of postwar novelists to fulfill their promise. An editorial in *Life Magazine* (September 12, 1955) describes the contemporary novelist as "an unemployed homosexual living in a packing-box shanty on the city dump while waiting admission to the county poorhouse" (21), and also bemoaned the context of present-day American fiction.

Steven Marcus, "The Novel Again," *Partisan Review*, XXIX (Spring, 1962), 171-95. Attacks "minor novelists" who are more concerned with form and poetry than with ideas. Stanley Edgar Hyman, "Some Trends in the Novel," *College English*, XX (October, 1958), 1-9. Hyman attacks "pseudo-fictions" and self parody of novelists. He has a similar view to that of Marcus.

3. Irving Howe, "Mass Society and Post-Modern Fiction," *Partisan Review*, XXVI (Summer, 1959), 420-36. Though Howe substantially agrees with Marcus and Hyman in their views (see note 2), he suggests a way out of the dilemma through the work of the "more serious of the 'post-modern' novelists—those who grapple with problems rather than merely betraying their effects—." These writers, he says, "have begun to envisage that we may be on the threshold of enormous changes in human history." Styron has moved steadily towards this confrontation in his work.

4. David L. Stevenson, "Styron and the Fiction of the Fifties," *Critique*, III (Summer, 1960), 56.

5. Ihab Hassan, *Radical Innocence* (Princeton, 1961), p. 5.

6. Peter Matthiessen and George Plimpton, "The Art of Fiction V" (interview with William Styron), *Paris Review*, V (Spring, 1954), 42-57. Reprinted in *Writers at Work: "The Paris Review" Interviews*, ed. with an introduction by Malcolm Cowley (New York, 1958), pp. 268-82. All future references will be to *Writers at Work*.

7. J. D. Scott, *New Statesman and Nation*, n.s. XLIII (April 19, 1952), 473.

8. R. A. Sokolov, "Into the Mind of Nat Turner," *Newsweek*, LXX (October 16, 1967), 67.

9. Eloise Perry Hazard, "Eight Fiction Finds," *Saturday Review of Literature*, XXV (February 16, 1952), 17.

10. Hazard, p. 17.

11. "Autumn"; "Long Dark Road," in *One and Twenty: Duke Narrative and Verse, 1924-1945*, ed. William M. Blackburn (Durham, North Carolina, 1945), pp. 36-53, 266-80.

12. Melvin J. Friedman, "William Styron: An Interim Appraisal," *English Journal*, L (March, 1961), 151.

13. "A Moment in Trieste," in *American Vanguard* (1948), ed. Don M. Wolfe (Ithaca, New York, 1948), pp. 241-47. (Published under the name "William C. Styron, Jr.")
"The Enormous Window," in *American Vanguard* (1950), ed. Charles I. Glicksberg (New York, 1950).

14. Cowley, p. 20.

15. William Styron, "Introduction," *Best Short Stories from "The Paris Review"* (New York, 1959), pp. 9-16.

16. William Styron, *"The Paris Review," Harper's Bazaar*, LXXXVII (August, 1953), 122-73.

17. Styron, "Introduction," p. 12.

18. *Ibid.*, p. 14.

19. "Writers Under Twenty-five," introductory essay to *Under Twenty-five: Duke Narrative and Verse, 1945-1962*, ed. William M. Blackburn (Durham, North Carolina, 1963), pp. 3-8.

20. "Writers Under Twenty-five," p. 6.

21. Tony Tanner, *The Reign of Wonder* (New York, 1967), pp. 12, 14.

22. David Dempsey, "Talk with William Styron," *New York Times Book Review* (September 9, 1951), p. 27. In this interview Styron stated of Mark Twain, "Hands down, he's the best writer we have produced." This statement should be considered in relation to Styron's propensities toward satire, and his continuing interest in the changing nature of American society.

23. *Set This House on Fire*, p. 10.

Chapter Two

1. Cowley, "The Faulkner Pattern," pp. 19-20.

2. *Writers at Work*, pp. 275-76.

3. Leslie Fiedler, *Waiting for the End* (London, 1965), p. 127.

4. Marvin Klotz, "The Triumph over Time: Narrative Form in William Faulkner and William Styron," *Mississippi Quarterly*, XVII (Winter, 1963-64), 9-20. This essay is the best study of Styron's structure.

5. In retrospect, Styron himself has been critical of the simultaneity of Peyton's suicide and the bombing of Hiroshima. Styron describes this coincidence as "gilding the lily." Perhaps he felt the symbolism interfered with his primary concern. In *Writers at Work*, p. 281, he says, "Really, I'm not trying to be rosy about things like the atom bomb and war and the failure of the Presbyterian Church. Those things don't alter one bit a writer's fundamental problems which are Love, Requited and Unrequited, Insult, et cetera."

6. Friedman, pp. 149-58, 192.

7. *Writers at Work*, p. 275.

8. *Writers at Work*, p. 282.

9. Maxwell Geismar, "William Styron: The End of Innocence," *American Moderns: From Rebellion to Conformity* (New York, 1958), p. 249.

10. *Writers at Work*, p. 281.

11. Nathanael West, "Some Notes on Miss Lonelyhearts," *Contempo*, III, 2 (May 15, 1933), 1.

12. *Writers at Work*, p. 281.

Chapter Three

1. Of the few critics who have related Styron's development through all his fiction, the most notable are: Jerry Bryant, "The Hopeful Stoicism of William Styron," *South Atlantic Quarterly*, LXII (Autumn, 1963), 539-50; Melvin J. Friedman, "William Styron: An Interim Appraisal," *English Journal*, L (March, 1961), 149-58, 192; David D. Galloway, *The Absurd Hero in American Fiction* (Austin, Texas, and London, 1966), pp. 51-81.

2. Maxwell Geismar, p. 243.

3. William Styron, "If You Write for Television . . . ," *New Republic*, CXL (April 6, 1959), 16.

4. Eugene McNamara, "Styron's *Long March:* Absurdity and Authority," *Western Humanities Review*, XV (Summer, 1961), 267-72.

5. All quotations are taken from William Styron's *The Long March*, Modern Library Paperback (Random House, 1956).

6. John Kuehl, ed., *Creative Writing and Rewriting: Contemporary American Novelists at Work* (New York, 1967), pp. 295-308. These pages contain a holograph of the first ten pages and the published version of those ten pages of *The Long March*.

7. William Styron, "MacArthur's Reminiscences," *New York Review of Books*, III (October 8, 1964), 3-5; a review of General Douglas MacArthur's Book.

8. Geismar, p. 248.

9. August Nigro, in *Critique*, IX (Winter, 1967), discusses Mannix's "rebellion in reverse." Mr. Nigro perceptively criticizes early essays on *The Long March* for missing the "mythic significance" in Styron's narrative. (Here he refers specifically to McNamara's interpretation.) He points out that Mannix is as brutalized and tyrannical as the system against which he rebels. Yet Mr. Nigro fails to note Culver's and Mannix's *recognition* of their true condition in the last scene of the novel, a scene which he never examines.

10. Galloway, pp. 63-64. Mr. Galloway never sees Mannix as a "super-marine" in his madness. He sees him only as a rebel figure. The real nature of Mannix's "absurdity" is not rebellion alone, or that the system cannot be overcome and that therefore his rebellion is pointless, but that the "System" is inside him. What he must do is to purge himself of the system, as do Cass Kinsolving and Nat Turner in Styron's later novels.

Chapter Four

1. David D. Galloway, "The Absurd Man as Tragic Hero: The Novels of William Styron," *The Absurd Hero In American Fiction* (Austin, Texas, 1966), pp. 51-81. The best analysis of Styron's philosophical position in the novel.

Lewis Lawson, "Cass Kinsolving: Kierkegaardian Man of Despair," *Wisconsin Studies in Contemporary Literature*, III (Fall, 1962), 54-

66. This article is one of the few thorough discussions of the philosophical basis of *Set This House on Fire*. Lawson associates Styron's novel with Christian Existentialism absorbed with the problems of despair and faith. The direct references and corollary ideas between Kierkegaard's *Sickness Unto Death* and *Set This House on Fire* indicate the possibility of the Danish philosopher's influence on Styron. However, the basic tone and mood of the novel are even more strongly affected by Styron's absorption with the religious imagery and intensity of John Donne. One of the aspects of Donne's holy sonnets and his sermons is the strong sense of the physical as well as spiritual despair, in addition to the violence of his language and imagery which he uses to overcome that despair. That sense of the physical is more valid in Donne's religious expression than in Kierkegaard's.

2. Arthur Mizener, "Some People of Our Time," *New York Times Book Review* (June 5, 1960), pp. 5, 26. Mizener only hints at the possibilities in the novel for Gothic satire but never elaborates on the subject.

3. *Newsweek* (October 16, 1967), p. 69. Styron was speaking of his last novel, *The Confessions of Nat Turner;* but, in retrospect, he saw rebellion as his central theme.

4. Several critics, judging the novel on its "realism," miss Styron's satiric approach. See Richard Foster, "An Orgy of Commerce: William Styron's *Set This House on Fire,*" *Critique,* III (Summer, 1960), 59-70.

5. Leslie Fiedler, *Love and Death in the American Novel* (Cleveland, 1962), pp. 418-19.

6. R. W. B. Lewis, *Trials of the Word* (Yale, 1965), p. 185.

7. "Mrs. Aadland's Little Girl, Beverly," *Esquire,* LVI (November, 1961), 142, 189-91. Review of Florence Aadland's *The Big Love;* reprinted in *First Person Singular,* ed. Herbert Gold (New York, 1965), pp. 209-16. "A fine and funny book," Styron calls West's novel.

8. French reviewers have been much more perceptive than American critics about *Set This House on Fire* as an American allegory rather than a tragedy. See André Bonnichon in "William Styron et le second Oedipe," *Etudes* (October, 1962), pp. 94-103. He refers to the novel as a "three fold psychological adventure . . . extended into the realm of allegory." What reference there is to Oedipus is

to the hero of *Oedipus at Colonus* who has purged himself of the poison of self-destruction.

9. Nathalia Wright, *American Novelists in Italy* (University of Pennsylvania Press, Philadelphia, 1965), p. 23.

10. Arthur Winner, "Adjustment, Tragic Humanism and Italy," *Studi Americani*, VII (1961), 311-61.

11. Louis D. Rubin, Jr., "An Artist in Bonds," *Sewanee Review*, LXIX (Winter, 1961), 174-79.

12. Cyril Arnovan, "Les romans de William Styron," *Europe*, XLI (September, 1963), 57.

13. Theodore Roethke, *Collected Poems* (New York, 1965), p. 108.

14. "The McCabes," *Paris Review*, XXII (Autumn-Winter, 1960), 12-28.

15. Albert Camus, *The Rebel* (New York, 1956), p. 105.

16. André Bonnichon, "William Styron et le second Oedipe." Although Bonnichon is generally interested in the Oedipus figures in Styron's work, he concentrates on the rebel figure's Oedipal problems. They exist in Mason Flagg's relation to his mother, as well as in all the Loftises in *Lie Down in Darkness*.

17. Heinz Politzer, *Franz Kafka: Parable and Paradox* (Ithaca, New York, 1962), pp. 216-17. Politzer sees K.'s last gesture in *The Trial* of spreading his fingers as ambiguously apt. K. both preserves "his humanity in an existential solitude" *and* accepts his judgment, welcoming death by the Court. Cass's *death* is accomplished by his murder-suicide of Mason Flagg and out of that action he achieves his redemption in existential "being."

18. Edwin Honig, *Dark Conceit: The Making of Allegory* (Cambridge, 1960), p. 159.

19. Galloway, p. 78.

20. Pierre Brodin, *Présences Contemporaines: Ecrivains Américains d'Aujourd'hui* (Paris, 1964), pp. 210-11.

21. Galloway, p. 73.

22. Nathaniel Hawthorne, *The Scarlet Letter* (New York, 1900), pp. 286-87. Hester tells Dimmesdale to free himself from his Puritan

guilt: "Begin all anew! Hast thou exhausted all possibility in the failure of this one trial? . . . Preach! Write! Act! Do anything save to lie down and die! Why shouldst thou tarry so much as one other day in the torments that have so gnawed into thy life!" Though not referring specifically to Hawthorne, Jean Baudrillard further developed this idea in a particularly perceptive article, "La Proie des Flammes," *Les Temps Modernes* (June, 1962), pp. 1928-37. He writes: "Above all Styron eliminates the theological or puritan hypothesis about evil: the slow elucidation of the murder reveals that we here no longer have an individual or racial fatality, or a personal one, but a shared manner of conduct, an exchange of guilts, a responsibility that has been lived through. One deserves one's fellow-man and he deserves you."

In Styron's novel, Luigi, like Hester with Dimmesdale, is trying to free Cass from the same intensely personal Puritan guilt so that he can relate again with other men. He must cut away the Dimmesdale in him and become like Hester. That is what Luigi means. See also R. W. B. Lewis's *The American Adam* (Chicago, 1955), pp. 110-26.

23. Alice R. Benson, "Techniques in the Twentieth Century Novel for Relating the Particular to the Universal: *Set This House on Fire*," *Papers of the Michigan Academy of Science, Arts and Letters*, XLVII (1962), 587-94. Miss Benson draws a parallel between Joyce's treatment of the *Odyssey* in *Ulysses* and Styron's reworking of *Oedipus at Colonus* in *Set This House on Fire*. Because of her interest in the tragic implications, she neglects the comic possibilities of such a comparison.

24. Michel Butor, "Oedipus Americanus," preface to *La Proie des Flammes* (Paris, 1962), p. xi.

25. Friedman, p. 192.

Chapter Five

1. John Aldridge, *Time to Murder and Create* (New York, 1966); Marvin Mudrick, "Mailer and Styron: Guests of the Establishment," *Hudson Review*, XVII (Autumn, 1964), 346-66. Both Aldridge and Mudrick refer to Styron as a "middlebrow" novelist. Aldridge's milder criticisms are directed against Styron's attempt to satisfy "middlebrow" tastes without confronting main issues. Mudrick, who sees Styron and Mailer as lionized by the American "establishment," criticizes their work as hollow and as conventionally safe.

2. Mike Thelwell, "Mr. Styron and The Reverend Turner," *Massachusetts Review*, IX (Winter, 1968), 29. This review-article later appears with nine other articles attacking Styron's novel in a collection entitled *William Styron's Nat Turner: Ten Black Writers Respond*, edited by John Henrik Clarke (Boston, 1968). There have been two articles written in rebuttal to the attack on Styron's novel: Martin Duberman's "Historical Fictions" in the *New York Times Book Review* (August 11, 1968), pp. 1, 16-17, and Eugene Genovese's "Nat Turner's Black Critics" in the *New York Review of Books*, XI (September 12, 1968), 34-37.

3. Dick Schaap, "Interview with William Styron," *Chicago Sun-Times Book Week* (October 8, 1967), p. 11.

4. Albert Camus, *The Rebel* (New York, 1956), pp. 265-66.

5. William Styron, "This Quiet Dust," *Harper's*, CCXXX (April, 1965), 134-46.

6. William Styron, "Overcome," *New York Review of Books*, III (September 26, 1963), 18.

7. Herbert Aptheker, *Negro Slave Revolts* (New York, 1963), pp. 193-324.

8. "This Quiet Dust," pp. 137-38.

9. Page Stegner and Robert Canzoneri, "An Interview with William Styron," *Per Se*, I (Summer, 1966), 37-44.

10. William Styron and James Jones, "Two Writers Talk It Over," *Esquire*, IX (July, 1963), 58.

11. "Overcome," p. 18.

12. Stanley Elkins, *Slavery* (Chicago, 1959), pp. 103-39.

13. "Overcome," p. 18.

14. Herbert Aptheker, *Nat Turner's Slave Rebellion* (New York, 1966), pp. 127-51.

15. "This Quiet Dust," p. 145.

16. Sigmund Freud, *The Interpretation of Dreams* (New York, 1961), p. 401.

17. A number of parallels can be drawn between Milton's hero in *Samson Agonistes* and Nat in the prison scenes. There are further

implications in Styron's image of Nat as a fly caught in Hell to Jonathan Edwards's view of "sinners in the hands of an angry God."

18. "Aftermath of Benjamin Reid," *Esquire*, LVIII (November, 1962), 79, 81, 158, 160, 164. "Death-in-life of Benjamin Reid," *Esquire*, LVII (February, 1962), 114, 141-45.

19. "Aftermath of Benjamin Reid," pp. 160.

20. Aptheker, *Nat Turner's Slave Rebellion*, pp. 127-51.

21. Louis D. Rubin, Jr., "William Styron and Human Bondage," *The Hollins Critic*, IV, 5 (December, 1967), 1-12.

22. Stegner and Canzoneri, "An Interview with William Styron," p. 41.

23. Alfred Kazin, *Book World, Chicago Tribune* (October 8, 1967), pp. 1, 22. Curtis Harnack, "The Quiddities of Detail," *The Kenyon Review*, XXX, 1 (1968), 125-32.

Chapter Six

1. Styron, "Mrs. Aadland's Little Girl, Beverly," *Esquire*, LVI (November, 1961), 190.

2. *Writers at Work*, p. 282.

3. Herbert Gold, "A Dog in Brooklyn, a Girl in Detroit: A Life Among the Humanities," *The Age of Happy Problems* (New York, 1962), pp. 118-38. Phillip Roth, "Writing American Fiction," *Commentary*, XXX (March, 1961), 223-33.

4. "Tootsie Rolls," *New York Review of Books*, II (May 14, 1964), 8.

5. "Controversy on Nat Turner Films," *San Francisco Chronicle* (March 19, 1968), p. 5. Howard Meyer, a New York attorney and biographer of Thomas Wentworth Higginson, cited an 1861 essay in the *Atlantic Monthly* in which Higginson clearly stated that Turner had a wife who was a slave to a different owner. Styron, in answer, pointed out that Higginson was reporting thirty years later. In another news story ("Styron Answers 'Turner' Critics," *New York Times* [February 11, 1968], p. 48), Styron stated in reference to Turner's wife that, in any case, "marriage during slavery was of course travesty."

6. *San Francisco Chronicle* (March 19, 1968), p. 5. In the article on *The Confessions of Nat Turner* in *Newsweek* (October 16, 1967), James Baldwin and Styron both consider Baldwin as a catalyst and as a partial model for Nat. The religious asceticism in Baldwin's own essays, autobiographical accounts, and novels lends support to this idea. A comparison of Nat's experiences with those of John Grimes in Baldwin's *Go Tell It on the Mountain* shows the connection in religious mood and theme.

7. Curtis Harnack, "The Quiddities of Detail," *Kenyon Review*, XXX, 1 (1968), 125-32. One of the best reviews of *The Confessions of Nat Turner*. Harnack sees how Styron fuses violent action with religious, sexual themes. He also sees the novel in its immediate sense as well as a meditation on history. Harnack's perceptive view should be contrasted with Stanley Kauffman's "Styron's Unwritten Novel," *Hudson Review* XX, 4 (Winter, 1967-68), 675-80. Kauffman misses the sexual-religious fusion and the significance of Nat's last scene in the cell. Kauffman spends some time on the "falseness" of Nat's language. There is some artificiality, but on the whole Styron keeps the tone and mood of the original confessions, a technique which may result in the "authorship" of which Kauffman complains.

8. "Two Writers Talk It Over," p. 58.

9. John Hope Franklin, *Chicago Sun-Times Book Week* (October 8, 1967), p. 2.

10. *San Francisco Chronicle* (March 19, 1968), p. 5.

11. *William Styron's Nat Turner: Ten Black Writers Respond,* ed. John Clark (Boston, 1968).

12. Eugene Genovese, "The Nat Turner Case," *New York Review of Books,* XI, 4, 34-37.

13. John Hope Franklin, as quoted in the *San Francisco Chronicle* (March 19, 1968), p. 5.

14. James Baldwin as quoted in *Newsweek* (October 16, 1967), p. 67.

15. Wm. Drewry, *Slave Insurrections in Virginia* (Washington: The Neal Co., 1900). Herbert Aptheker, *Nat Turner's Slave Rebellion* (New York, 1966).

16. *San Francisco Chronicle* (March 19, 1968), p. 5. William Strickland, writer, as quoted in an interview.

17. "Two Writers Talk It Over," p. 59.

18. Franz Fanon, *The Wretched of the Earth* (New York, 1968). Though Fanon's book deals primarily with former colonies emerging as national states, the attitudes of the formerly exploited masses toward their former masters parallel the feelings of Styron's slaves in *The Confessions of Nat Turner*. In fact, this is his social theme.

Chapter Seven

1. Styron has a recognized standing among French critics particularly. He, like Faulkner, is concerned with social and individual morality. Combining satirical and philosophical themes, he has an especial appeal to the French.

2. John M. Bradbury, *Renaissance in the South* (Chapel Hill, North Carolina, 1963), pp. 196-202; C. Vann Woodward, *The Burden of Southern History* (Baton Rouge, Louisiana, 1960), p. 21. Both these social historians are particularly helpful in providing background to the changing conditions in Southern life.

3. Wright Morris, "The Territory Ahead," *The Living Novel* (New York, 1957), pp. 120-56.

4. Harriet Doar, "Interview with William Styron," *Red Clay Reader*, Vol. I (1964), p. 26.

5. David Dempsey, "Talk with William Styron," *New York Times Book Review* (September 9, 1951), p. 27.

6. *Writers at Work*, p. 272.

7. John Aldridge, *New York Times Book Review* (September 9, 1951), p. 5. Mr. Aldridge has modified his views in his new book, *Time to Murder and Create* (New York, 1966), pp. 30-51. In his essay on Styron, Mr. Aldridge makes the distinction between Faulkner's world and Styron's. Faulkner's people are lost because they have been wrenched out of a natural place in the commercial order, an order which does not exist in Styron's chaotic world. By implication, Aldridge is describing the end of tragedy. Styron has made this one of his themes in all of his fiction: tragic figures operating outside of a tragic framework. The main point here is that Aldridge has changed his view about Styron as a regional writer.

8. F. J. Hoffman, "The Sense of Place," *South* (New York, 1961), p. 68.

9. Malcolm Cowley, *New Republic,* CXXV (October 8, 1951), 19-20.

10. Walter Sullivan, "The Continuing Renascence," *South* ed. Louis D. Rubin, Jr., and Robert D. Jacobs (New York, 1961), p. 389.

11. Louis D. Rubin, Jr., "William Styron: Notes on a Southern Writer in Our Time," *The Faraway Country* (Seattle, Washington, 1963), pp. 185-230.

12. Doar, *Red Clay Reader,* p. 26.

13. Brodin, *Présences Contemporaines* (Paris, 1964), pp. 210-11.

14. Morris, "The Territory Ahead," p. 145.

15. *Ibid.,* p. 146.

16. "Writers Under Twenty-five," p. 7.

Selected Bibliography

PRIMARY SOURCES

(Listed in chronological order by types.)

1. Novels

Lie Down in Darkness. Indianapolis, Ind.: Bobbs-Merrill, 1951; London: Hamish Hamilton, 1952.
Set This House on Fire. New York: Random House, 1960, London: Hamish Hamilton, 1961.
The Long March. London: Mayflower, 1961; New York: Vintage, 1962.
The Confessions of Nat Turner. New York: Random House, 1967; London: Jonathan Cape, 1968.

2. Short Stories

"Autumn." William M. Blackburn, ed. *One and Twenty: Duke Narrative and Verse, 1924-1945.* Durham, N.C.: Duke University Press, 1945.
"The Long Dark Road." In William M. Blackburn, ed. *One and Twenty: Duke Narrative and Verse, 1924-1945.* Durham, N.C.: Duke University Press, 1945.
"A Moment in Trieste." In Don Wolfe, ed. *American Vanguard.* Ithaca, N.Y.: Cornell University Press, 1948.
"The Enormous Window." In Charles I. Glicksberg, ed. *1950 American Vanguard.* New York: New School for Social Research, 1950.
"The Long March." In John W. Aldridge and Vance Bourjaily, eds. *Discovery No. 1.* New York: Pocket Books, 1953. Collected as *The Long March.* Reprinted: *The Best Short Stories of World War II: An American Anthology*, Charles Fenton, ed. New York: Viking Press, 1957.
"The McCabes." *Paris Review,* XXII (Autumn-Winter, 1959-60), 12-28. Incorporated into *Set This House on Fire* as part of Chapter VI.
"Works in Progress." *Esquire,* LX (July 1963), 50-51, 105. Incorporated into *The Confessions of Nat Turner.*
"Virginia: 1831." *Paris Review,* IX (Winter 1966), 13-45. Incorporated into *The Confessions of Nat Turner* as part of Chapter I.

"Runaway." *Partisan Review*, XXII (Fall 1966), 574-82.
"The Confessions of Nat Turner." *Harper's*, CCXXXV (September 1967), 51-102. Incorporated into *The Confessions of Nat Turner.*
"Novel's Climax: The Night of the Honed Axes." *Life*, LXIII (October 13, 1967), 54-60. Incorporated into *The Confessions of Nat Turner.*

3. Articles

"Letter to an Editor." *Paris Review*, I (Spring, 1953), 9-16.
"Prevalence of Wonders." *The Nation*, CLXXVI (May 2, 1953), 370-71.
"*The Paris Review.*" *Harper's Bazaar*, LXXXVII (August, 1953), 122, 173.
"What's Wrong With the American Novel?" *American Scholar*, XXIV (Autumn, 1955), 464-503 [Roundtable discussion with Ralph Ellison, Hiram Haydn, *et al*].
"If You Write for Television . . . . " *New Republic*, CXLVI (April 6, 1959), 16.
"Introduction." In *Best Short Stories From "The Paris Review."* New York: E. P. Dutton, 1959.
"Mrs. Aadland's Little Girl, Beverly," *Esquire*, LVI (November 1961), 142, 189-91. Reprinted: *First Person Singular: Essays for the Sixties*, Herbert Gold, ed. New York: Dial Press, 1963. Pp. 209-16. Reprinted as "True Confessions.": *Esquire's World of Humor.* New York: Esquire, 1964.
"The Death-in-Life of Benjamin Reid." *Esquire*, LVII (February, 1962), 141-45. Reprinted: *An Approach to Literature.* 4th ed. Cleanth Brooks, John Thibaut Purser, and Robert Penn Warren, eds. New York: Appleton-Century-Crofts, 1964.
"As He Lay Dead, A Bitter Grief." *Life*, LIII (July 20, 1962), 39-42.
"Aftermath of Benjamin Reid." *Esquire*, LVIII (November, 1962), 79.
"Writers Under Twenty-five." William M. Blackburn. ed. *Under Twenty-five: Duke Narrative and Verse, 1945-1962.* Durham, N.C.: Duke University Press, 1963.
"Two Writers Talk It Over." *Esquire*, LX (July, 1963), 57-59 [Discussion with James Jones].
"This Quiet Dust." *Harper's*, CCXXX (April, 1965), 135-46. Reprinted: *Best Magazine Articles of the Year 1966*, Gerald Walker, ed. New York: Crown Publishers, 1966.

"Truth and Nat Turner: An Exchange—William Styron Replies." *Nation*, CCVI (April 22, 1968), 544-47.

"Oldest America." *McCall's*, XCV (July, 1968), 94, 123.

"Symposium: Violence in Literature." *American Scholar*, XXXVII (Summer, 1968), 482-96 [Roundtable with Robert Penn Warren, Theodore Solotaroff, Robert Coles, and Styron].

"In the Jungle." *New York Review of Books*, XI (September 26, 1968), 11-13.

"My Generation." *Esquire*, LXX (October, 1968), 123-24.

"On Creativity." *Playboy*, XV (December, 1968), [Styron's statement appears on p. 138.]

"The Uses of Historical Fiction." *Southern Literary Journal*, I (Spring 1969), 57-90 [Discussion with Ralph Ellison, Robert Penn Warren, C. Vann Woodward, and Styron].

4. Book Reviews and Record Review

"New Editions." *New York Review of Books*, I (Special Issue, 1963), 43 [*Slave and Citizen: The Negro in the Americas*, by Frank Tannenbaum].

"Overcome." *New York Review of Books*, I (September 26, 1963), 18-19 [*American Negro Slave Revolts*, by Herbert Aptheker].

"An Elegy for F. Scott Fitzgerald." *New York Review of Books*, I (November 28, 1963), 1-3 [*The Letters of F. Scott Fitzgerald*, Andrew Turnbull, ed.].

"The Habit." *New York Review of Books*, I (December 26, 1963), 13-14 [*The Consumers Union Report on Smoking and the Public Interest*, Ruth and Edward Brecher, eds.].

"A Southern Conscience." *New York Review of Books*, II (April 2, 1964), 3 [*A Southern Prophecy*, by Lewis H. Blair].

"Tootsie Rolls." *New York Review of Books*, II (May 14, 1964), 8-9 [*Candy*, by Terry Southern and Mason Hoffenberg].

"MacArthur." *New York Review of Books*, II (October 8, 1964), 3-5 [*Reminiscences*, by Douglas MacArthur].

"John Fitzgerald Kennedy . . . as we remember him." *High Fidelity*, XVI (January, 1966), 38. ["John Fitzgerald Kennedy . . . as we remember him," by Charles Kuralt: Columbia Recording L2L:1017].

"The Vice That Has No Name." *Harper's*, CCXXXVI (February, 1968), 97-100 [*Light on Dark Corners . . .*, by B. G. Jefferis and J. L. Nichols].

"The Shade of Thomas Wolfe," *Harper's*, CCXXXVI (April, 1968), 96, 98-104 [*Thomas Wolfe*, by Andrew Turnbull].

SECONDARY SOURCES

ALDRIDGE, JOHN W. *After the Lost Generation.* New York: McGraw-Hill, 1951. This study of postwar novelists compares them with the major writers of the 1920's and 1930's.
————. "The Society of Three Novels." *In Search of Heresy.* New York: McGraw-Hill, 1956. An early study of Styron's *Lie Down in Darkness* emphasizing Styron's "regionalism."
————. "William Styron and the Derivative Imagination." *Time to Murder and Create.* New York: David McKay, Inc., 1966. A revised view of Styron; regards his work as quite distinctive from Faulkner's and other Southern writers.

APTHEKER, HERBERT. *American Negro Slave Revolts.* New York: International Publishers, 1963. Documented account of slave revolts; argues that there was a great, incessant restiveness among slave populations in the South.
————. *Nat Turner's Slave Rebellion.* New York: Humanities Press, 1966. Specific account of the Turner Rebellion with an appendix containing the original confessions.
————. "A Note on the History," *Nation,* CCV (October 16, 1967), 375-76. Attack on the historical accuracy of Styron's *Confessions of Nat Turner.*

ARNAVON, CYRILLE. "Les romans de William Styron," *Europe,* XLI (September, 1963), 54-66. Excellent article which concentrates on *Set This House on Fire* and its social allegory.

BAUDRILLARD, JEAN. "La proie des flammes," *Temps Modernes,* CXCIII (1962), 1928-37. On *Set This House on Fire,* particularly on the Puritan versus humanistic struggle in the novel.

BAUMBACH, JONATHAN. "Paradise Lost: The Novels of William Styron," *South Atlantic Quarterly,* CXIII (Spring, 1964), 207-17. Collected in *The Landscape of Nightmare* (New York: New York University Press, 1965), 123-37. Fairly comprehensive study of Styron's work, emphasizing his apocalyptic descriptions. Writing mainly about *Lie Down in Darkness,* Baumbach sees Styron's work primarily as a description of the "degeneration of contemporary civilization."

BENSON, ALICE R. "Techniques in the Twentieth-Century Novel for Relating the Particular to the Universal: *Set This House on Fire,*" *Papers of the Michigan Academy of Science, Arts and Letters,* XLVII (1962), 587-94. Miss Benson draws a parallel between Joyce's treatment of the *Odyssey* in *Ulysses* and Styron's reworking of *Oedipus at Colonus* in *Set This House on Fire*. Because of her interest in the tragic implications, she neglects the comic possibilities of such a comparison.

BONNICHON, ANDRÉ. "William Styron et le second Oedipe," *Etudes*, XIII (October, 1962), 94-103. Although Bonnichon is generally interested in the main characters as Oedipus figures in Styron's work, he concentrates on the rebel figure's Oedipal problems. These problems also exist in Mason Flagg's relation to his mother, as well as in all the Loftises in *Lie Down in Darkness*.

BRADBURY, JOHN M. *Renaissance in the South*. Chapel Hill: University of North Carolina Press, 1963. Particularly helpful in providing material on the changing conditions in the twentieth-century South.

BRIERRE, ANNIE. "La Proie des Critiques," *Nouvelles Littéraires*, XL (March 22, 1962), 8. Interview of Styron by his translators, Maurice Coindreau and Michel Butor.

BRODIN, PIERRE. *Présences Contemporaines: Ecrivains Américains d'Aujourd'hui*. Paris: Les Nouvelles Editions Debresse, 1964. Brief analyses of some contemporary American writers and some valuable correspondence on French influences on their work.

BRYANT, JERRY H. "The Hopeful Stoicism of William Styron," *South Atlantic Quarterly*, LXII (Autumn, 1963), 539-50. One of the earliest, best comprehensive studies of Styron's work.

BUTOR, MICHEL. Preface, *La Proie des Flammes*. Paris: Gallimard, 1963. Important statement from one of the most significant of the new French novelists; develops the Oedipal theme in *Set This House on Fire*.

CANZONERI, ROBERT, and PAGE STEGNER. "An Interview with William Styron," *Per Se*, I (Summer, 1966), 37-44. Key interview; Styron expresses his views on *The Confessions of Nat Turner*.

CLARK, JOHN, ed. *William Styron's Nat Turner: Ten Black Writers Respond*. Boston: Beacon Press, 1968. Ten essays attacking Styron's *Confessions of Nat Turner* as a racist account of historical fact.

DAVIS, ROBERT GORHAM. "In a Ravelled World Love Endures," *New York Times Book Review* (December 26, 1954), pp. 1, 13. Discussion of postwar writers, their concerns and values.

————. "Styron and the Students," *Critique*, III (Summer, 1960), 37-46. Discussion of Styron's descriptive techniques and his tendency toward excessive hyperbole.

————. "The American Individualist Tradition: Bellow and Styron." *The Creative Present*. Eds. Norma Balakian and Charles Simmons. New York: Doubleday, 1963. On the limitations of the self in Styron's and Bellow's works.

DETWEILER, ROBERT. "William Styron and the Courage To Be." *Four Spiritual Crises in Mid-Century American Fiction*. Gainesville: University of Florida Press, 1964. Generalized discussion of Styron's religious and philosophical views.

DOAR, HARRIET. "Interview with William Styron," *Red Clay Reader*, I (1964), 26-30. Excellent interview; reveals much about influences on Styron and his approach to fiction.

DREWRY, WILLIAM SIDNEY. *Slave Insurrections in Virginia*. Washington: The Neal Company, 1900. Segregationist source of information on Nat Turner's Rebellion, used by Styron for some factual details.

DUBERMAN, MARTIN. "Historical Fictions," *New York Times Book Review* (August 11, 1968), I, 26-27. Strongly critical review of Clarke's *Ten Black Writers*.

ELKINS, STANLEY M. *Slavery: A Problem in American Institutional and Intellectual Life*. Chicago: University of Chicago Press, 1959. Major source of and influence on *The Confessions of Nat Turner*.

FENTON, CHARLES A. "William Styron and the Age of the Slob," *South Atlantic Quarterly*, LIX (Autumn, 1960), 469-76. Early assessment of Styron's work.

FIEDLER, LESLIE. *Love and Death in the American Novel*. New York: Criterion Books, 1960. Critical study of fiction in America, particularly of the cultural attitudes toward sexuality and death, guilt and freedom, and the way in which the Gothic and sentimental modes of the novel have been employed by American novelists.

FINKELSTEIN, SIDNEY. "Cold War, Religious Revival and Family Alienation: William Styron, J. D. Salinger and Edward Albee." *Existentialism and Alienation in American Literaure*. New York: International Publishers, 1965. Comparative essay on moral and social issues with main emphasis on *Lie Down in Darkness*.

Selected Bibliography

FOSTER, RICHARD. "An Orgy of Commerce: William Styron's *Set This House on Fire*," *Critique*, III (Summer, 1960), 59-70. Adversely critical of *Set This House on Fire*; attacks the style which is dominated by Cass's mind as "vulgar" and "sentimental." Mr. Foster admits the "ostensible self-satire," but he feels that it "always turns into misty-eyed, self-admiring whimsy." I believe Mr. Foster does not consider the influence of Luigi, and to some extent that of Leverett on Cass. Cass resembles Gulliver in several ways; to take his views literally as Styron's is to miss the satiric intent of the novel.

FRIEDMAN, MELVIN J. "William Styron: An Interim Appraisal," *English Journal*, L (March, 1961), 149-58, 192. Perceptive, useful assessment of Styron's work linking *Set This House on Fire* with French writers of the Existential school.

FRIEDMAN, MELVIN J., and IRVING MALIN, eds. *William Styron's* THE CONFESSIONS OF NAT TURNER: *A Critical Handbook*. Belmont, California: Wadsworth Publishing Company, Inc., 1970. All of the essays in this collection are listed in my bibliography as appearing elsewhere with the exception of two essays, "William Styron's Clown Show" by Roy Arthur Swanson, and "William Styron's *Divine Comedy*" by Karl Malkoff. Both essays deal primarily with *Set This House on Fire*. Mr. Swanson's essay is an attack on the language and "pretense" of the novel. Mr. Malkoff is much more favorably disposed toward Styron's objectives and results. The authors have included a very comprehensive bibliography, and the collection itself is a valuable introduction, not only to the problem of Styron's *The Confessions of Nat Turner*, but to the question of Styron's artistic ability as well.

FRIEDMAN, MELVIN J., and AUGUST J. NIGRO, eds. *Configuration Critique de William Styron*, Paris: Minard, 1967. A collection of essays by French and American critics of Styron.

GALLOWAY, DAVID D. "The Absurd Man as Tragic Hero: The Novels of William Styron," *Texas Studies in Language and Literature*, VI (Winter, 1965), 512-34. Reprinted in *The Absurd Hero in American Fiction: Updike, Styron, Bellow, Salinger*. Austin and London: University of Texas Press, 1966. Excellent development of Styron's interest in contemporary French literature, particularly of Camus's work and the influences evident in his first three novels.

GEISMAR, MAXWELL. "William Styron: The End of Innocence," *American Moderns: From Rebellion to Conformity*. New York: Hill and Wang, 1958. Good early assessment of Styron; emphasizes his motifs of children, innocence, and infantile behavior in *Lie Down in Darkness.*

GENOVESE, EUGENE. "The Nat Turner Case," *New York Review of Books*, XI, 4 (September 12, 1968), 34-37. Best critical argument answering Clarke's collection of essays.

GILMAN, RICHARD. "Nat Turner Revisited," *New Republic*, CLVIII (April 27, 1968), 23-32. Attack on *The Confessions of Nat Turner* from a literary standpoint. Misses the point that the landscape and weather are not there to give a sense of versimilitude but to present Nat Turner's sense of the natural and social worlds.

GOSSETT, LOUISE Y. *Violence in Recent Southern Fiction.* Durham, North Carolina: Duke University Press, 1965. Discussion and comparison of the use of violence as a reflection of social change in Faulkner, O'Connor, Styron, and others.

GROSS, SEYMOUR and EILEEN BENDER, "The Myth of Nat Turner", *American Quarterly*, XXIII (October, 1971), 487-518. A comprehensive summary and analysis of factual and imaginative treatments of Nat Turner. Strongly supports Styron's imaginative approach.

HASSAN, IHAB. "Encounter with Necessity." *Radical Innocence.* Princeton: Princeton University Press, 1961. Section on Styron reprinted in Richard Kostelanetz's (ed.) *On Contemporary Literature.* New York: Avon Books, 1964. Pp. 597-606. Early view of Styron in the context of post-war American fiction.

HAYS, PETER L. "The Nature of Rebellion in *The Long March*," *Critique*, VIII, (Winter, 1965-66), 70-74. Brief examination of the novella.

HAZARD, ELOISE PERRY. "Eight Fiction Finds," *Saturday Review of Literature*, XXXV (February 16, 1952), 17. Early comparison of Styron and other new writers.
————. "William Styron," *Saturday Review of Literature*, XXXIV (September 15, 1951), 12. Early interview with Styron with some biographical details.

HOFFMAN, FREDERICK J. "The Cure of 'Nothing': The Fiction of William Styron." *Frontiers of American Culture.* Eds. Ray B. Browne, Richard H. Crowder, Virgil L. Lokke, and William T. Stafford. Lafayette, Indiana: Purdue University Studies, 1968.

————. "The Sense of Place." *South*. Eds. Louis D. Rubin, Jr., and Robert D. Jacobs. Garden City, New York: Doubleday, 1961. Southern atmosphere reflected in fiction.

HONIG, EDWIN. *The Dark Conceit*. Cambridge, Massachusetts: Walker de Berry Inc., 1960. Excellent study of allegory and its relation to satire and other forms.

HOWE, IRVING. "Mass Society and Post-Modern Fiction," *Partisan Review*, XXVI (Summer, 1959), 420-36. Discussion of the problems of modern fiction writers. Perceptive views on limitations of "beat" writers withdrawn from society and praise for the "serious" writers "who grapple with problems rather than merely betray their effects."

KAYSER, WOLFGANG. *The Grotesque in Art and Literature*. Trans. Ulrich Weisstein. Bloomington: Indiana University Press, 1963. Major study of the grotesque as a form from its development in the middle ages to the 1920's. Particularly useful in reference to *Set This House on Fire*.

KLEIN, MARCUS. *After Alienation*. Cleveland: Meridian Books, 1962. Studies of postwar fiction. Klein presents his ideas on alienation and accommodation of post-World War II writers. His ideas are useful in examining the themes and ideas of Styron's contemporaries and their break with the idea of the alienated hero.

KLOTZ, MARVIN. "The Triumph Over Time: Narrative Form in William Styron," *Mississippi Quarterly*, XVII (Winter, 1963-64), 9-20. Excellent comparative essay showing Faulkner's and Styron's use of time in *The Sound and the Fury, Absalom, Absalom!, Lie Down in Darkness*.

KUEHL, JOHN, ed. *Creative Writing and Rewriting, Contemporary American Novelists at Work*. New York: Appleton-Century-Crofts, 1967. Contains portions of original manuscript of *The Long March*.

LAWSON, JOHN H. "Styron: Darkness and Fire in the Modern Novel," *Mainstream*, XIII (October, 1960), 9-18. On Styron's apocalyptic vision of twentieth-century America.

LAWSON, LEWIS. "Cass Kinsolving: Kierkegaardian Man of Despair," *Wisconsin Studies in Contemporary Literature*, III (Fall, 1962), 54-66. Study of *Set This House on Fire* from the perspective of Christian Existentialism.

LEHAN, RICHARD. "Existentialism in Recent American Fiction: The Demonic Quest," *Texas Studies in Language and Literature,* I (Summer, 1959), 181-202. Excellent discourse on some American versions of the Existentialist quest, particularly in Bowles, Bellows, and Ellison. *Set This House on Fire* is mentioned briefly. The essay is the most provocative on the subject of American interpretations of the Existential dilemma.

LEMAIRE, MARCEL. "Some Recent American Novels and Essays," *Revue des Langues Vivantes,* XXVIII (January-February, 1962), 70-78. Fairly good but brief discussion of *Set This House on Fire.*
————. *The American Adam.* Chicago: University of Chicago Press, 1955. Basic study of the Adamic figure in nineteenth- and twentieth-century American literature.
————. *Trials of the Word.* New Haven: Yale University Press, 1965. Collection of essays. Most useful in discussions on the apocalyptic viewpoint in American letters.

LICHENSTEIN, GERALD. "The Exiles," *New Statesman and Nation,* n.s. XLIX (September 6, 1958), 320-22. Invaluable analysis of the *Paris Review* group, their significance, and their occasional pretentiousness.

LUDWIG, JACK. *Recent American Novelists.* Minneapolis: University of Minnesota Press, 1962. General discussion of post-World War II novelists. Compares Styron's work with his contemporaries'.

MACKIN, COOPER R. *William Styron.* Southern Writer Series, No. 7. Austin, Texas: Steck-Vaughn Company, 1969. This pamphlet is written primarily from the point of view of Styron as a Southern writer. Some interesting parallels are drawn between Styron's heroes as Southern rebels.

MAILER, NORMAN. "Norman Mailer vs. Nine Writers," *Esquire,* LX (July, 1963), 63-69, 105. Mailer's criticism of *Set This Houe on Fire* as a novel that does not make it.

MARCUS, STEVEN. "The Novel Again," *Partisan Review,* XXIX (Spring, 1962), 171-95. Criticism of new fiction as "minor."

MATTHIESSEN, PETER, and GEORGE PLIMPTON. "The Art of Fiction V" (interview with William Styron), *Paris Review,* V (Spring, 1954), 42-57. Reprinted in *Writers at Work: "The Paris Review" Interviews.* Ed., with an introduction by, Malcolm Cowley. New York: Viking, 1958. Key interview about Styron's views on postwar fiction. He discusses his own work, *Lie Down in Darkness*— particularly his approach to the technique of the novel.

Selected Bibliography

McNamara, Eugene. "Styron's *Long March*: Absurdity and Authority," *Western Humanities Review*, XV (Summer, 1961), 267-72.
Interpretation of Styron's *Long March* as a novel of acceptance
and order.
————. "The Post-Modern American Novel," *Queen's Quarterly*,
LXIX (Summer, 1962), 265-75. General survey of contemporary
fiction with particular emphasis on Styron.

Meeker, Richard K. "The Youngest Generation of Southern Fiction
Writers." *Southern Writers: Appraisals in Our Time*. Ed. R. C.
Simo. Charlottville, Virginia: University of Virginia Press, 1958.
Discussion of Styron's place in contemporary Southern fiction.

Mizener, Arthur. "Some People of Our Time," *New York Times
Book Review* (June 5, 1960), 5, 26. Valuable review of *Set This
House on Fire*.

Mohrt, Michel. "Le Renouveau du Roman Psychologique." *Le Nouveau Roman Américain*. Paris: Gallimard, 1955. Early French
appraisal of Styron.

Monaghan, Charles. "Portrait of a Man Reading" (interview), *Chicago Tribune Book World* (October 27, 1967), p. 8. Gives an
important listing of Styron's background reading for his work.
Includes his experience with Elizabethan literature and the influence of Faulkner, Flaubert, and Gide, as well as a number of
praiseworthy comments about contemporary writers.

Moore, L. Hugh. "Robert Penn Warren, William Styron, and the Use
of Greek Myth," *Critique*, VIII (Winter, 1965-66), 75-87. Compares Styron's and Robert Penn Warren's uses of Greek myths.
Believes Warren's use of myth as source is more effective than
Styron's use of Classical drama.

Morris, Wright. "The Territory Ahead." *The Living Novel*. Ed.,
Granville Hicks. New York: Macmillan Co., 1957. Wright's projections for the future of the novel in America are valuable for
an understanding of what Styron and other new novelists are
attempting.

Mudrick, Marvin. "Mailer and Styron: Guests of the Establishment,"
Hudson Review, XVII (Autumn, 1964), 346-66. Highly critical
of Styron and Mailer for making a commercial appeal to "middlebrow" readers whose guides and mentors are the New York literary establishment.

NIGRO, AUGUST. *"The Long March.* The Expansive Hero in a Closed World," *Critique,* IX, 3 (Winter, 1967), 103-12. Perceptive essay on the novella.

NYREN, DOROTHY, ed. "William Styron." *A Library of Literary Criticism.* New York: Frederick Ungar, 1964. Some general biographical information on Styron.

O'CONNELL, SHAWN. "Expense of Spirit: The Vision of William Styron," *Critique,* VIII (Winter, 1965-66), 9-33. Good comprehensive survey of Styron's development from personal tragedy to social consciousness. Very good on *Lie Down in Darkness* and *Set This House on Fire.*

O'CONNOR, WILLIAM VAN. "John Updike and William Styron: The Burden of Talent." *Contemporary American Novelists.* Ed., Harry T. Moore. Carbondale: Southern Illinois University Press, 1964. Pretty thin article on first three novels. Main point seems to be that "Styron simply has no subject; he has enormous talent in search of a subject."

RATNER, MARC L. "Styron's Rebel," *American Quarterly,* XXI (Fall, 1969), 595-608. A condensed version of Chapter V; about *The Confessions of Nat Turner.*

————. "The Rebel Purged," *Arlington Quarterly,* II (Autumn, 1969), 27-42.

————. "Rebellion of Wrath and Laughter: Styron's *Set This House on Fire,*" *Southern Review,* VII (Autumn, 1971), 1007-1020.

ROBB, KENNETH A. "William Styron's Don Juan," *Critique,* VIII (Winter, 1965-66), 34-46. Further development of the Kierkegaardian viewpoint in *Either/Or.* The Don Juan theme and the Mozartian motif are clearly related to events in *Set This House on Fire.* But the idea of parody and satire suggested by Richard Foster and several French critics is never developed here.

ROTH, PHILIP. "Writing American Fiction," *Commentary,* XXXI (March, 1961), 222-33. This key essay on the dilemma of the fiction writer attempts to describe the grotesqueries and chaos of postwar American life.

RUBIN, LOUIS D., JR., and ROBERT D. JACOBS, eds. "Introduction: Southern Writing and the Changing South." *South.* Garden City, New York: Doubleday, 1961. Valuable background study to the social and psychological changes taking place in the South. Styron reflects these changes in his fiction.

————. "The South and the Faraway Country," *Virginia Quarterly Review,* XXXVIII (Summer, 1962), 444-59. On social change in the South.

Selected Bibliography

————. "William Styron and Human Bondage," *The Hollins Critic,* IV, 5 (December, 1967), 1-12. Key review of *The Confessions of Nat Turner.* Rubin sees Nat as the latest in a series of Styron's heroes attempting to free himself from social bondage.

————. "William Styron: Notes on a Southern Writer in our Time," *The Faraway Country.* Seattle: University of Washington Press, 1963. Enlargement of Styron's role in the new literature of the South.

STEVENSON, DAVID L. "Fiction's Unfamiliar Face," *Nation,* CLXXXVII (November 1, 1958), 307-9.

————. "Novelists of Distinction." *The Creative Present.* Eds., Norma Balakian and Charles Simmons, 195-212. Significance of Styron, Bellow, and others as new novelists who are influenced by European writers and philosophers.

————. "Styron and the Fiction of the Fifties," *Critique,* III (Summer, 1960), 47-58. Reprinted in *Recent American Fiction: Some Critical Views.* Ed. Joseph J. Waldmeir. New York: Houghton Mifflin Company, 1963. Early appreciation of Styron.

TANNER, TONY. *The Reign of Wonder.* New York: Cambridge University Press, 1965. Discussion of naïveté and reality in American nineteenth-century writers.

THELWELL, MICHAEL. "Mr. Styron and the Reverend Turner," *Massachusetts Review,* IX (Winter, 1968), 7-29. Well-written essay attacking Styron's *Confessions of Nat Turner.* Included in Clarke essays.

THELWELL, MICHAEL and ROBERT COLES. "Nat Turner," *Partisan Review,* XXXV (Summer, 1968), 403-14. Exchange of views on the novel.

THORP, WILLARD. "The Southern Mode," *South Atlantic Quarterly,* LXIII (Autumn, 1964), 576-82. Styron as a regional writer and as derivative of Faulkner.

URANG, GUNNAR. "The Broader Vision: William Styron's *Set This House on Fire,*" *Critique,* VIII (Winter, 1965-66), 47-69. Theme of guilt and judgment in *Set This House on Fire.*

WALDMEIR, JOSEPH. "Quest Without Faith," *Nation,* CXCIII (November 18, 1961), 390-96. On *Set This House on Fire* briefly and on the contemporary fictional hero, committed to action but on personal not social terms.

WINNER, ARTHUR. "Adjustment, Tragic Humanism and Italy," *Studi Americani, VII* (Rome, Italy) (1961), 311-61. On some American writers in Italy; long section on *Set This House on Fire.*

WOODWARD, C. VANN. *The Burden of Southern History.* Baton Rouge: Louisiana State University Press, 1960. The Southern historical past as an element influencing contemporary writers, Faulkner, Warren, and Styron.

WRIGHT, NATHALIA. *American Novelists in Italy.* University of Pennsylvania Press, 1965. Primarily on nineteenth-century American writers who set their novels in Italy. Excellent background for *Set This House on Fire* on the conflict between Puritanism and humanism.

Index

(The works of William Styron are listed under his name)